The UVM Primer

Books by Ray Salemi

Leading After a Layoff
(McGraw Hill)

FPGA Simulation
(Boston Light Press)

Robot Haiku
(Adams Media)

Ray Salemi also writes mystery fiction as Ray Daniel
(www.raydanielmystery.com)

Terminated
(Midnight Ink, August 2014)

Uber-Geek Tucker and his beautiful wife Carol developed top-secret spy software together until the day he was fired and she was murdered. Haunted by his dead wife, Tucker is determined to track down her killer—no matter what the cost. Office politics turn deadly as Tucker takes on the FBI, Russian mobsters, and a psychopath known as the Duct Tape Killer.

The UVM Primer

An Introduction to the Universal Verification Methodology

Ray Salemi

For Karen, who brings out the best in me.

Table of Contents

Table of Figures

Acknowledgements

It would have been impossible to write and deliver a clear and accurate book on the Universal Verification Methodology (UVM) without the help of many people.

Thank you to Mentor Graphics for providing the software and technical support that made it possible to deliver the runnable code examples in this book. My coworkers at Mentor Graphics were gracious about answering questions that came up in the writing of the book. I'd particularly like to thank Dave Rich for straightening me out on handles vs. pointers, Joe Rodriguez for his review and feedback, and Tom Fitzpatrick for his invaluable copyediting skills and ability to catch places where my code examples didn't match my words.

Thank you also to Von Wolff and Kari Ross for reading initial drafts of The UVM Primer and providing me with valuable suggestions.

Chapter 1

Introduction

PRIMER—An elementary textbook that serves as an introduction to a subject of study.
(New Oxford American Dictionary)

As a verification consultant and expert using the Universal Verification Methodology (UVM), I'm often asked, "What book should I read to learn the UVM?"

The question has had me flummoxed because, while there are many good online references for the UVM[1] there has never been a book that teaches the reader the UVM in a simple fashion from first principles.

Until now.

The **UVM Primer** is the book to read when you've decided to learn the UVM. The book assumes that you have a basic knowledge of SystemVerilog and the principles of verification, and takes you step-by-step from that starting point to the point where you can write and understand UVM-based testbenches.

Short and Sweet

The **UVM Primer** is a concise introduction to the UVM. I wrote it so that the average verification engineer could read it quickly enough to prepare for a job interview. The book features short chapters, lots of examples, and an easy-to-read style.

I've avoided the boring philosophical questions normally associated with an introductory book ("What is the history of the UVM?" "Who wrote the UVM?" "Can I use the UVM to make a delicious flan?").

The **UVM Primer** gives you everything you need to understand and write a UVM Testbench, without delving into all UVM's nooks and crannies. The UVM is huge, and a book that covered the whole thing would be enormous. Instead, the **UVM Primer** gives you the concepts you need to investigate the features of the UVM on your own.

What Are These "Concepts" of Which You Speak?

The UVM builds upon the following simple concepts:

- SystemVerilog Object-Oriented Programming

- Dynamically-generated objects that allow you to specify tests and testbench architecture without recompiling

---

[1] You can see a list of these references at www.uvmprimer.com along with a downloadable version of all the code examples in this book.

[2] The source code for the TinyALU is included with the sample code available at www.uvmprimer.com.

[3] I provide an introduction to covergroups in the book *FPGA Simulation*.

- A hierarchical testbench organization that includes Agents, Drivers, Monitors, and Bus Functional Models

- Transaction-level communication between objects

- Testbench stimulus (UVM Sequences) separated from the testbench structure

By the end of the book you will have a firm grasp of each of these concepts and how they contribute to your testbenches.

Online Components

The *UVM Primer* discusses the UVM through code. This presents a challenge to the reader and author in terms of the detailed code discussion. On the one hand, a line-by-line description of the code is boring. On the other hand, a high-level discussion of a code snippet's behavior can leave some readers scratching their heads as to how the code implements what is promised. These details should not be left as an exercise to the reader.

I've addressed this problem by supplementing high-level discussions of code behavior in the book with detailed videos available through www.uvmprimer.com. A video is available for each chapter's code example.

People reading a primer are bound to have additional questions about the topic. You can ask these questions on the *UVM Primer* Facebook page. This is a central location for readers to discuss the book's concepts and code examples.

You can download the code examples from www.uvmprimer.com either as a gzipped tar file or as a pull from a GIT repository on www.git-hub.com.

Example Design

We will examine the UVM by verifying a simple design: the TinyALU. By doing this, we can focus our energy on the testbench without getting distracted by DUT complexity.

The TinyALU is a simple ALU written in VHDL. It accepts two eight-bit numbers (A and B) and produces a 16-bit result. Here is the top level of the TinyALU[2]:

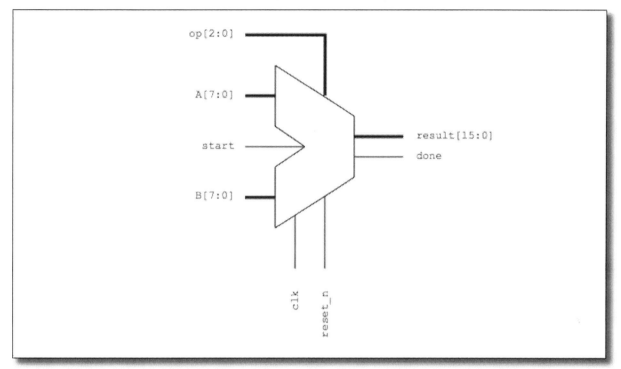

Figure 1: TinyALU Block Diagram

The ALU works at the rising edge of the clock. When the `start` signal is active, the TinyALU reads operands off the A and B busses and an operation off the `op` bus, and delivers the result based on the operation. Operations can take any number of cycles. The TinyALU raises the `done` signal when the operation is complete.

The `reset_n` signal is an active-low, synchronous reset.

---

[2] The source code for the TinyALU is included with the sample code available at www.uvmprimer.com.

The TinyALU has five operations: NOP, ADD, AND, XOR, and MULT. The user encodes the operations on the three bit op bus when requesting a calculation. Here are the encodings:

Operation	Opcode
no_op	3'b000
add_op	3'b001
and_op	3'b010
xor_op	3'b011
mul_op	3'b100
unused	3'b101-3'b111

Figure 2: TinyALU Operations and Opcodes

Here is the waveform for the TinyALU:

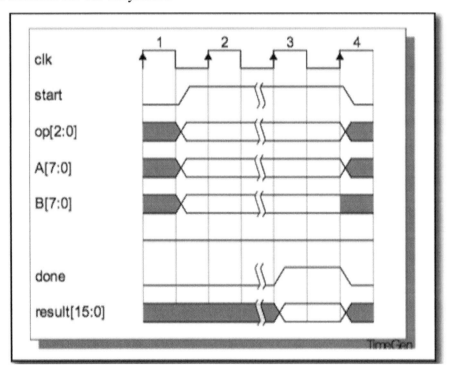

Figure 3: TinyALU Protocol Waveform

The start signal must remain high, and the operator and operands must remain stable until the TinyALU raises the done signal. The done signal stays high for only one clock. There is no done signal on a NOP operation. On a NOP, the requester lowers the start signal one cycle after raising it.

We'll start our journey through the UVM by creating a conventional testbench of the TinyALU. Then each chapter will modify the testbench to make it UVM compliant. We'll discuss the advantages of using the UVM as we transform the testbench.

A Note on the Code Font

Talking about code forces us to mention variable names. Since these can be confusing in a sentence (e.g., "waiting for start to go high"), I will use `this code font` to identify variables and SystemVerilog keywords (e.g., "waiting for `start` to go high").

Chapter 2

A Conventional Testbench for the TinyALU

It is easier to learn something new if we start from something familiar. In this case, we're going to start from a traditional SystemVerilog testbench. Once we have the traditional testbench in place, we're going to modify it, step-by-step, until it is a complete UVM testbench.

Our testbench for the TinyALU needs to do the following:

- Completely test the TinyALU's functionality
- Simulate all the lines of RTL and the paths through those lines

This is a "coverage first" methodology. We define what we want to cover, and we create a testbench that covers it.

We will create a self-checking testbench so that we can run regressions without having to examine the results manually.

The TinyALU Functional Coverage Model

We'll use SystemVerilog covergroups to implement the TinyALU coverage model. While we won't go into the details of the covergroups in this book[3], here are the coverage goals:

- Test all operations
- Simulate all zeros on an input for all operations
- Simulate all ones on an input for all operations
- Execute all operations after a reset
- Run a multiply after a single cycle operation
- Run a single cycle operation after a multiply
- Simulate all operations twice in a row

We can be sure that our TinyALU is working if we've tested all these scenarios and not gotten any errors. We'll also check that we've got 100% code coverage. We will not be discussing coverage in detail beyond this chapter, so you can skip over the covergroup definitions if you like.

---

[3] I provide an introduction to covergroups in the book *FPGA Simulation*.

The Testbench File

We store the TinyALU testbench in one simulation file. The file contains three parts: stimulus, self-checking, and coverage. We instantiate the DUT in the file, and drive its signals with the stimulus while monitoring it with the self-checking and coverage `always` blocks.

Testbench Variable Declarations

First, we define the operations for the TinyALU in a way that allows us to easily define stimulus. Then we declare all the signals in our testbench:

```
1   module top;
2
3       typedef enum bit[2:0] {no_op  = 3'b000,
4                              add_op = 3'b001,
5                              and_op = 3'b010,
6                              xor_op = 3'b011,
7                              mul_op = 3'b100,
8                              rst_op = 3'b111} operation_t;
9       byte        unsigned        A;
10      byte        unsigned        B;
11      bit         clk;
12      bit         reset_n;
13      wire [2:0]  op;
14      bit         start;
15      wire        done;
16      wire [15:0] result;
17      operation_t op_set;
18
19      assign op = op_set;
20
21      tinyalu DUT (.A, .B, .clk, .op, .reset_n, .start, .done, .result);
22
23
```

Figure 4: Testbench Declarations and Instantiations

We use the SystemVerilog enumerated type to define the TinyALU operations as enumerations. We have added the `rst_op` enumeration for testbench convenience, as the DUT doesn't use this opcode. The `assign` statement applies the opcode to the DUT's op bus.

We define the stimulus variables using SystemVerilog types such as `byte` and `bit`. Finally, we instantiate the DUT using a nifty SystemVerilog feature that matches ports to signals without needing to type the single name twice.

The `coverage` Block

We've defined our functional coverage model in terms of stimulus. The TinyALU is fully tested if we've run a complete set of stimulus through it.

We'll use covergroups to capture functional coverage. We declare the covergroups, instantiate them, and use them for sampling. First, let's look at the definitions:

```
24
25      covergroup op_cov;
26
27          coverpoint op_set {
28              bins single_cycle[] = {[add_op : xor_op], rst_op,no_op};
29              bins multi_cycle = {mul_op};
30

45      covergroup zeros_or_ones_on_ops;
46
47          all_ops : coverpoint op_set {
48              ignore_bins null_ops = {rst_op, no_op};}
49
50          a_leg: coverpoint A {
51              bins zeros = {'h00};
52              bins others= {['h01:'hFE]};
53              bins ones  = {'hFF};
54          }
```

Figure 5: TinyALU Covergroup Definitions

These definitions show some of the bins in the coverage model.[4] The `op_cov` covergroup makes sure that we've covered all the operations and the possible interactions between them. The `zeros_or_ones_on_ops` covergroup checks to see if we've had all zeros and all ones on the data ports and that we've tested all operations with these combinations.

Once we've defined the covergroups we need to declare, instantiate, and sample them:

```
111     initial begin : coverage
112
113         oc = new();
114         c_00_FF = new();
115
116         forever begin @(negedge clk);
117             oc.sample();
118             c_00_FF.sample();
119         end
120     end : coverage
121
```

Figure 6: Declaring, Instantiating, and Sampling Covergroups in the `coverage` Block

This is a very simple coverage model. We examine the operations and data inputs on the TinyALU at the negative edge of every clock and record what we see.

---

[4] These covergroups are discussed in more detail in videos on www.uvmprimer.com.

To jump to the end of the story, this testbench achieves 100% functional coverage:

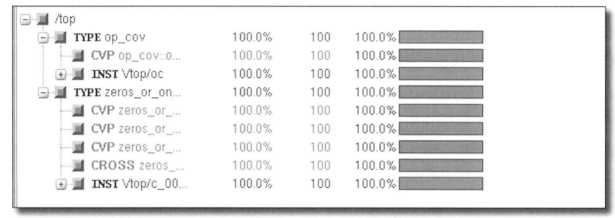

Figure 7: Complete Functional Coverage[5]

This complete coverage comes from our constrained random stimulus.

The `tester` Block

In a perfect world, we would write a directed test for every coverage goal. In the case of the TinyALU, that's possible, but it's more coding than necessary. Instead, we'll create randomized stimulus. Since purely random stimulus can be incorrect and mostly uninteresting, we'll constrain the stimulus to legal, interesting values.

We'll implement our constrained-random stimulus using two functions: `get_op()` and `get_data()`:

```
168     initial begin : tester
169        reset_n = 1'b0;
170        @(negedge clk);
171        @(negedge clk);
172        reset_n = 1'b1;
173        start = 1'b0;
174        repeat (1000) begin
175           @(negedge clk);
176           op_set = get_op();
177           A = get_data();
178           B = get_data();
179           start = 1'b1;
180           case (op_set) // handle the start signal
181              no_op: begin
182                 @(posedge clk);
183                 start = 1'b0;
184              end
```

Figure 8: The `tester` Block Creates Constrained Random Stimulus

---

[5] This is a screen shot from Mentor Graphics' Questa Verification Platform. Mentor Graphics owns the copyright to this and all screenshots of Questa's GUI or output formats and has given me permission to reprint them in this book.

This loop generates 1000 transactions for the TinyALU. Each time through the loop we get a random operation from `get_op()` and random data from `get_data()`, drive them to the TinyALU, and handle the protocol of the `start` signal. These functions ensure that we get legal operations and interesting data. They are discussed in detail later in the book.

Notice how many different things we do in this block. We choose the number of operations, choose the data, and manage the signal-level protocol. Later in the book we will use the TinyALU to generate the Fibonacci sequence. Imagine how difficult it would be to modify this testbench to create that test. For one thing, we'd have to completely rewrite this block.

Self-Checking with the Scoreboard Loop

The scoreboard loop checks the actual TinyALU results against predicted results. The loop watches the `done` signal. When the `done` signal goes high, the scoreboard predicts the TinyALU output based on the inputs and checks that the output is correct:

```
149    always @(posedge done) begin : scoreboard
150       shortint predicted_result;
151       case (op_set)
152          add_op: predicted_result = A + B;
153          and_op: predicted_result = A & B;
154          xor_op: predicted_result = A ^ B;
155          mul_op: predicted_result = A * B;
156       endcase // case (op_set)
157
158       if ((op_set != no_op) && (op_set != rst_op))
159          if (predicted_result != result)
160             $error ("FAILED: A: %0h  B: %0h  op: %s result: %0h",
161                      A, B, op_set.name(), result);
162
163    end : scoreboard
```

Figure 9: The `scoreboard` Block

We Have a Testbench

We have successfully completed the TinyALU testbench. Our testbench delivers functional coverage, checks that all the operations work properly, and required very little work in stimulus generation. It delivered all of this in one module and one file.

Yet this is a poor example of a testbench. All the behavior is jumbled together in one file. This jumbling makes the testbench difficult to reuse or build upon.

How do we improve this testbench? The first thing we notice is that the scoreboard block, the coverage block, and the tester block each define completely different pieces of functionality. They shouldn't be in the same file. By separating them, we'll be able to reuse portions of the testbench in other testbenches and easily modify parts of the testbench such as the stimulus.

In our next chapter, we'll break our testbench up into modules and we'll learn about how to use a SystemVerilog Interface as a bus functional model (BFM).

Chapter 3

SystemVerilog Interfaces and Bus Functional Models

In the last chapter we created a pretty good testbench for the TinyALU. It featured all the elements of a modern testbench:

- Functional Coverage Goals—The testbench measures what we've tested rather than relying upon a list of tests.

- Self-Checking—We don't have to examine waveforms or look at text output. We can run as many tests as we like.

- Constrained Random Stimulus—We didn't have to write tests for all the operations; we simply created random stimulus that fulfilled the coverage requirements.

The downside of our testbench was its lack of modularity. All the functionality was crammed into one file and one SystemVerilog module. This makes it difficult to modify, reuse, or debug that testbench. This is a design flaw.

Verification teams have two choices. They can either design testbenches that get more buggy and brittle as the project grows, or they can design testbenches that get more adaptable and powerful as the design grows.

The testbench we wrote in the previous chapter is the former. Because all its functionality is crammed into one file, that testbench will not grow gracefully with a design. Instead we'll have to keep hacking new pieces onto it, or copying it and modifying it, or worst of all, using `#ifdefs` to control what gets compiled from simulation to simulation.

By the time our project gets into crunch time, we'll have a testbench that's so brittle that nobody dares touch it because it breaks at the slightest modification.

Then, even if we do get through the project, we'll find it almost impossible to use this confusing, brittle, buggy monstrosity on our next design.

Who needs that?

Instead, engineers need a standardized way to create modular testbenches that grow more powerful over time. We want a testbench that grows stronger each time we add a resource and gives future developers easy ways to mix and match features to create new functionality.

Fortunately, SystemVerilog gives us the tools to do the job. The SystemVerilog *interface* is the first of these tools. SystemVerilog interfaces encapsulate the port signals in a testbench and make it easy to share those signals between modules and, as we'll see, objects.

Our first step on the road to the UVM is to modularize our testbench using SystemVerilog interfaces. We'll see that interfaces allow us to go beyond simply sharing signals. We can also use them to create a Bus Functional Model, and thus encapsulate the protocol associated with a bus in simple access routines.

The TinyALU BFM (Bus Functional Model)

The `tinyalu_bfm` encapsulates all the signals in the TinyALU testbench and provides a clock, a `reset_alu()` task, and a `send_op()` task that sends an operation to the TinyALU. We define a SystemVerilog interface in the same way that we define a module. We start with the `interface` keyword and define the signals in the interface:

```
1   interface tinyalu_bfm;
2       import tinyalu_pkg::*;
3
4       byte        unsigned    A;
5       byte        unsigned    B;
6       bit         clk;
7       bit         reset_n;
8       wire [2:0]  op;
9       bit         start;
10      wire        done;
11      wire [15:0] result;
```

Figure 10: The TinyALU BFM: Signals and Clock

The BFM provides our first step towards modularization. It handles all the signal-level stimulus issues so that the rest of our testbench can ignore these issues. For example, the `tinyalu_bfm` generates the clock. This modularization provides immediate benefits when we break the testbench into modules.[6]

The BFM provides two tasks: `reset_alu()` and `send_op()`. Here is `reset_alu()`:

```
25      task reset_alu();
26          reset_n = 1'b0;
27          @(negedge clk);
28          @(negedge clk);
29          reset_n = 1'b1;
30          start = 1'b0;
31      endtask : reset_alu
```

Figure 11: Task to Reset the ALU

The `reset_alu()` task drops the reset signal, waits a couple of clocks, and raises it again.

---

[6] The `tinyalu_pkg` defines the `operation_t` enumerated type that we will see below. It is discussed in more detail in the videos.

The `send_op()` task sends an operation into the ALU and returns the results:

```
33    task send_op(input byte iA, input byte iB, input operation_t iop,
34                 output shortint alu_result);
35
36        op_set = iop;
37
38        if (iop == rst_op) begin
39            @(posedge clk);
```

Figure 12: The `send_op()` Task Definition

The type `operation_t` is an enumerated type defined in the package `tinyalu_pkg`. We imported `tinyalu_pkg` at the top of the interface.

The `send_op()` task demonstrates how a BFM encapsulates the protocols associated with a DUT:

```
45        end else begin
46            @(negedge clk);
47            A = iA;
48            B = iB;
49            start = 1'b1;
50            if (iop == no_op) begin
51                @(posedge clk);
52                #1;
53                start = 1'b0;
54            end else begin
55                do
56                    @(negedge clk);
57                while (done == 0);
58                start = 1'b0;
59            end
```

Figure 13: Encapsulating the TinyALU Signal-Level Protocols

In this case, the task places an operation on the op bus and data on the operand busses. Then it raises the `start` signal and lowers it based upon the operation requested. Encapsulating this behavior has two benefits:

- We don't need to sprinkle our code with protocol-level behavior; code that calls this task is simpler than code that would have to handle the signals.

- We can modify all the protocol level behavior in one place; a fix here gets propagated throughout the design.

Now that we have a TinyALU BFM, we can modularize the rest of the design.

Creating a Modular Testbench

Now that we've got a BFM, we can create modules that implement our three testbench operations (tester, scoreboard, and coverage) and connect them to the DUT through the BFM:

```
1   module top;
2      tinyalu_bfm    bfm();
3      random_tester     random_tester_i    (bfm);
4      coverage   coverage_i  (bfm);
5      scoreboard scoreboard_i(bfm);
6
7      tinyalu DUT (.A(bfm.A), .B(bfm.B), .op(bfm.op),
8                   .clk(bfm.clk), .reset_n(bfm.reset_n),
9                   .start(bfm.start), .done(bfm.done), .result(bfm.result));
10     endmodule : top
11
```

Figure 14: Connecting Testbench Modules with a BFM

The benefit of breaking the testbench into modules jumps out immediately. Not only is the coder's intent blindingly obvious, but we also know where to go if we want to fix or enhance any part of the testbench. The testbench has four parts:

- tinyalu_bfm—A SystemVerilog interface that contains all the signal-level behavior
- tester—A module that generates the test stimulus
- coverage—A module that provides functional coverage
- scoreboard—A module that checks the results

We pass the SystemVerilog interface to a module when we instantiate it. The only signal-level connections in the testbench happen at the DUT. You can see that the DUT instantiation references the signals inside the BFM.

We are going to implement this basic four-part architecture through the book as we convert this testbench into a UVM testbench. We've taken each of the loops from our previous testbench and encapsulated them into modules.

As an example of turning a loop into a module, here is the `scoreboard`:

```
1   module scoreboard(tinyalu_bfm bfm);
2       import tinyalu_pkg::*;
3
4       always @(posedge bfm.done) begin
5           shortint predicted_result;
6           case (bfm.op_set)
7               add_op: predicted_result = bfm.A + bfm.B;
8               and_op: predicted_result = bfm.A & bfm.B;
9               xor_op: predicted_result = bfm.A ^ bfm.B;
10              mul_op: predicted_result = bfm.A * bfm.B;
11          endcase // case (op_set)
12
13          if ((bfm.op_set != no_op) && (bfm.op_set != rst_op))
14              if (predicted_result != bfm.result)
15                  $error ("FAILED: A: %0h  B: %0h  op: %s result: %0h",
16                          bfm.A, bfm.B, bfm.op_set.name(), bfm.result);
17
18      end
19  endmodule : scoreboard
20
```

Figure 15: The Complete `scoreboard` Module

We access the signals in the BFM by using `bfm` in a hierarchical reference. The rest of the logic is the same as the loop from the monolithic testbench.

The tester module is simpler now because it no longer has to manage signal-level protocols. It calls the BFM tasks instead:

```
36          bfm.reset_alu();
37          repeat (1000) begin : random_loop
38              op_set = get_op();
39              iA = get_data();
40              iB = get_data();
41              bfm.send_op(iA, iB, op_set, result);
42          end : random_loop
43          $stop;
44      end // initial begin
45  endmodule : tester
```

Figure 16: Using the BFM in the `tester` Module

Summary of Bus Functional Models

In this chapter we broke our monolithic testbench into easily manageable, logical pieces. The testbench has four compilation units now: the `tinyalu_bfm` interface along with `tester`, `scoreboard`, and `coverage` modules.

In the next chapters, we'll implement this basic four-piece architecture using object oriented programming? Why? Because object-oriented programming provides powerful tools for writing and maintaining complicated testbenches.

We will spend the next six chapters learning about object-oriented programming, and then we'll start using the UVM.

Chapter 4

Object-Oriented Programming (OOP)

When people think of Steve Jobs making his fateful visit to Xerox PARC in the 1970s, they imagine him making off with the crown jewels: the window/keyboard/mouse interface that made the Macintosh famous.

The thing is, Steve Jobs later recalled that PARC showed him two things beyond the mouse that would prove to be game changers. One was computer networking. The other was object-oriented programming. When Scully banished Jobs from Apple, Jobs created a company called NeXT Computer with the intention of bringing object-oriented programming to market. The world's first web servers and browsers were written using NeXT's libraries.

Object-oriented programming (OOP) took off in the 1990s with the advent of languages such as C++ and Java. Soon everybody would be learning to program using OOP. (If you teach your kids to program, start them on object-oriented programming.)

Verification engineers also started using object-oriented programming in the 1990s. At first this was done by linking C++ into a Verilog simulator. The testbench could be written with OOP and then the DUT was driven through the PLI. Meanwhile Verisity was launching the e language. e built upon object-oriented programming to deliver aspect-oriented programming and soon became the premier verification language.

Elsewhere in 1997, the folks at Co-Design were adding object-oriented extensions to Verilog to create a new language called Superlog. Co-Design donated Superlog to the industry standards group Accellera. Accellera combined Superlog with another donated language, Vera, to create SystemVerilog.

Why All This OOP Love?

Software engineers and verification engineers love object-oriented programming for three reasons:

- Code Reuse
- Code Maintainability
- Memory Management

Let's look at each of these in turn.

Code Reuse

Consider a simple microcontroller. A chip such as this contains a microprocessor, registers, a UART and other interfaces. You don't need to know how the designer implemented these, you only need to know the definition of the waveforms at the pins and the opcodes. In fact, you can use the same microcontroller code whether your microcontroller is delivered to you in its own package, as part of a chip, or even programmed into an FPGA.

The same is true of objects in object-oriented programming. Programming objects contain data and tasks and functions that operate on that data. Once you have a defined object, you don't need to worry about what's inside it; you simply need to use it as the documentation tells you to use it.

Reuse means that your testbench becomes more powerful with every function you add. If you program your new functionality correctly, you can use it to create more new functionality building upon your previous work.

Code Maintainability

Every time you copy a piece of code from one part of your testbench to another, you are creating a potential code maintenance disaster. You want the code to be identical in both places, but if you find a bug in one location, you need to search through your program to fix it everywhere.

The problem gets even worse if you copy someone else's code. In that case, they'll fix a bug in their code but probably won't tell you about the fix. Now you're out of sync.

Object-oriented programming does away with this problem. You write common code in one place and access it from all over your testbench. If you leverage code written by another person, you will automatically benefit from changes made to that person's code.

Properly written object-oriented code is easy to maintain.

Memory Management

As we learn about object-oriented programming, we'll find ourselves creating objects and passing them around the testbench. What we're really doing is allocating memory and sharing it between threads in our program. This is a painful and bug-ridden process in traditional languages such as C, but it is easy in pure object-oriented programming languages such as SystemVerilog and Java. It's so easy that we don't even know we're doing it.

Summary of Object-Oriented Programming

Object-oriented programming is an enormous subject. OOP books can, and do, fill entire bookcases. As cool as object-oriented programming is, we won't be delving into all its nooks and crannies in this book. Instead, we're going to learn just enough about object-oriented programming to use the UVM effectively.

Still, that encompasses some powerful object-oriented concepts. We'll get started by talking about classes and extension.

Chapter 5

Classes and Extension

Let's say we're on a long car drive. We decide to play twenty questions, and I go first. I tell you that I'm thinking of an animal. You tell me that an animal is a foolish choice because you don't need twenty questions to guess it, but I persist. You roll your eyes, bet me a beer that you can guess my animal in ten questions, and start.

"What phylum?" you ask, and I realize that I've been snookered.

I try the "That's not fair" argument for a bit, but a bet is a bet, so I tell you that the phylum is "Chordata." Now you know that my animal has a backbone.

"What class?"

"Mammalia."

Now you know that my animal has hair, milk glands, and a hammer, anvil and stapes in its middle ear.

"Order?"

"Rodentia."

It has large front teeth that grow continuously.

"Family?" you ask.

"Family?" I respond. "I don't know the family."

"How are we supposed to play if you can't answer questions about your animal?"

I fish around on my smart phone, find Wikipedia and read, "Muridae. But from now on, you have to guess for real."

You know it's a small rodent with a slender body, a long tail, and a pointed snout.

You try some guesses. "Squirrel?" "No." "Rat?" "No." "Mouse?"

"Yes. I owe you a beer."

Our guessing game demonstrates one of the most powerful concepts in life science, that of classification. Classification is a shorthand way of capturing information about the wide variety of life on our planet.

The same is true with software objects.

Object-oriented programming uses classification to enforce code reuse. If I tell you that an animal is a rodent, then you know a lot about it because you know about rodents. Similarly, if I tell you that a software object is a certain class, then you know its capabilities.

Start with Structs

We're going to approach classes by moving from the familiar (structs) to the unfamiliar (classes). Consider two structs that we'll use to hold data about geometric shapes: rectangles and squares.

```
1   typedef struct {
2       int         length;
3       int         width;
4   } rectangle_struct;
5
6   typedef struct {
7       int         side;
8   } square_struct;
```

Figure 17: Structs for Rectangles and Squares

We see that structs do a pretty good job of capturing all the information about a rectangle and a square. We use that information below to store and print information about these shapes:

```
10  module top_struct ;
11      rectangle_struct rectangle_s;
12      square_struct        square_s;
13    initial begin
14      rectangle_s.length = 50;
15      rectangle_s.width  = 20;
16      $display("rectangle area: %0d", rectangle_s.length * rectangle_s.width);
17      square_s.side = 50;
18      $display("square area: %0d", square_s.side ** 2);
19    end
20  endmodule
```

Figure 18: Using Our Rectangle and Square Structs

I declared a variable of type `rectangle_struct` and type `square_struct`, then I stored dimensions into these variables and used them to calculate area.

Here are some facts about these structs:

- Though we know there is a relationship between rectangles and squares, our program does not.

- The simulator allocated the memory for the rectangle and square as soon as we declared the variables.

- It is impossible to calculate the area of the rectangle and square if the user doesn't know the equation. This might become a bigger issue if we wanted to capture trapezoids or rhomboids.

Let's rewrite our rectangle as a class and see how classes address these issues.

Defining a Class

Here is a rectangle defined as a class. We will use this example to define some object-oriented terms:

```
1    class rectangle;
2       int length;
3       int width;
4
5       function new(int l, int w);
6          length = l;
7          width  = w;
8       endfunction
9
10      function int area();
11         return length * width;
12      endfunction
13   endclass
14
```

Figure 19: Defining the `rectangle` Class

The first thing to notice is that we use the `class` keyword to define a class. Unlike the struct in Figure 17 we do not use curly braces to encase the class; we use the `endclass` keyword instead.

We have declared class variables called `length` and `width`. In object-oriented terms these are called the class's *data members*. Most classes contain data members.

We have defined a function, `area()`, that uses the data members to return the rectangle's area. This function is available to anyone with access to this rectangle class. We call a function or a task defined within a class a **method**. We say, "The rectangle class has two data members, `length` and `width`, and a method called `area`."

The simulator treats classes differently from structs when it comes to allocating memory. While the simulator allocates memory for structs as soon as they are declared, it does not do the same for classes. The user must explicitly allocate the memory for an object by calling the class's constructor method: `new()`.

In this example we've defined `new()` so that it requires the user to provide a length and width. It makes no sense for someone to create a rectangle without these attributes, and we want to catch such errors at compile time rather than at runtime.

We use the class in a module like this:

```
23    module top_class ;
24      rectangle rectangle_h;
25      initial begin
26        rectangle_h = new(.l(50),.w(20));
27        $display("rectangle area: %0d", rectangle_h.area());
28      end
29    endmodule
```

Figure 20: Using the `rectangle` Class

The first thing we did was declare a variable of type `rectangle`. We call the variable `rectangle_h` to show that it holds a ***handle*** to a rectangle. A handle is similar to a memory handle, except it does not allow handle arithmetic. This declaration set aside enough memory to store the handle. It did not allocate the memory for the object.

We allocate the memory for the object when we call `new()` and create a `rectangle` with a length of 50 and a width of 20. (The dots in the function call are just old fashioned Verilog. We are explicitly attaching the numbers to the values in the constructor rather than relying upon the argument order.) This is called ***instantiating*** the object. We say, "Instantiated an object of class `rectangle` and stored it in a variable called `rectangle_h`."

The number of objects we instantiate is limited only by the amount of memory in our computer. We can copy the handles to these rectangles into other variables, we can store handles in arrays, and we can pass them around a testbench to control our simulation.

SystemVerilog handles all the memory allocation while we are manipulating objects. It gives us new memory for objects when we call `new()` and it recovers memory from objects when we stop referencing them. For example, if we had created a second rectangle and stored it in the `rectangle_h` variable, the simulator would have recovered the memory from our first rectangle object.

Now that we have a `rectangle` object stored in the variable `rectangle_h`, we can use the `area()` method to calculate the area of our rectangle. We do that within the `$display()` statement:

```
23    module top_class ;
24      rectangle rectangle_h;
25      initial begin
26        rectangle_h = new(.l(50),.w(20));
27        $display("rectangle area: %0d", rectangle_h.area());
28      end
29    endmodule
```

Figure 21: Letting the Rectangle Calculate Its Area

This simple example demonstrates how object-oriented programming allows engineers to use each other's code without needing to understand the implementation. The engineer using the rectangle object needs only to supply the length and width upon creation and call the `area()` method. The thinking behind the object has been done by the person who defined the class.

The `rectangle` class demonstrates the basics of defining a class. Next we'll look at another critical feature of object-oriented programming: extension.

Extending Classes

In our original struct-based example (Figure 18), we defined a struct to hold rectangles and another struct to hold squares. There wasn't much reuse possible between these structs. If we created an `area()` function that took a `rectangle_struct` struct as an argument, it would not be able to take a `square_struct` struct as an argument, and if we created an `area()` function that took length and width as arguments, we would be defeating the purpose of the encapsulation.

Object-oriented programming solves this reuse problem with the same approach we saw in our mouse guessing game: progressive and more detailed classification. We can build SystemVerilog classes upon each other just as we built the Rodentia order upon the Mammalia class.

In this example, we note that a square is a rectangle whose sides are the same length. That means we can reuse the concepts of length and width and area. We capture that reusability with the `extends` keyword:

```
15    class square extends rectangle;
16
17      function new(int side);
18        super.new(.l(side), .w(side));
19      endfunction
20
21    endclass
```

Figure 22: Defining the `square` Class

The code above completely defines the `square` class. The keyword `extends` tells the compiler that, by default, the `square` class uses all the data members and methods defined in the `rectangle` class.

The only exception is cases where we *override* the data member or method by defining it in this class. In this case, we've *overridden* the constructor `new()`. The `square`'s version of `new()` has only one argument: the length of the side. It takes that side, and then it does something unique to object-oriented programming. It calls `super.new()`.

The `super` keyword tells the compiler to explicitly reference the data member or method defined in this class's parent class. In the case of the `square`, the super keyword in `new()` tells the simulator that we want to call the constructor in `rectangle` and pass it `side` as the length and width.

We are completely reusing the code from the `rectangle` class without having to copy it or even look at it. We take advantage of the fact that a `square` is a specialized case of a `rectangle` and let the compiler do the work. Here is our code in action:

```
27      initial begin
28
29          rectangle_h = new(.l(50),.w(20));
30          $display("rectangle area: %0d", rectangle_h.area());
31
32          square_h = new(.side(50));
33          $display("square area: %0d", square_h.area());
34
35      end
36  endmodule
```

Figure 23: Using the `square_h` Object

We declare a variable of type `square` and call `new()` to create a new object. We call `new()` twice, but we are actually running different versions of `new()`: one inside of `rectangle` and the other inside of `square`. This is a convention of SystemVerilog (and many other languages). The compiler understands that all calls to `new()` relate to the type of the variable on the left-hand side of the assignment.

The `square`'s area method acts just like the `rectangle`'s area method because they are running the same code.

Summary of Classes and Extension

The ability to define classes based upon other classes and to create a topography of functionality is the key feature that differentiates object-oriented programming from more traditional forms of programming. When you combine this with the ability to create multiple copies of objects, you get a powerful platform for creating software and testbenches.

Yet this is just the beginning. Thinking more deeply about objects and their classifications leads you to a new world of powerful programming techniques. Consider: The above example has a variable called `rectangle_h` and an object of type `square`. Since a `square` is a `rectangle`, should we be able to store a `square` in the `rectangle_h` variable?

Yes, we can. This is called polymorphism, and we'll look at it in the next chapter.

Chapter 6

Polymorphism

Object-oriented programming lends itself to big words. Normally these words could be replaced with simpler words. ***Instantiation*** could have been ***creation***. ***Design Patterns*** could have been ***Programming Tricks***. ***Polymorphism*** could have been . . . well, maybe nothing else. It is unique to object-oriented programming.

Polymorphism springs from the fact that object-oriented class types are derived from each other. A square is a rectangle is a parallelogram is a trapezoid is a polygon. It causes one to ask, "If I declare a variable of type polygon and I instantiate a square object, can I store the square object in my polygon variable?" The answer is yes, and that language behavior is called polymorphism.

Let's examine polymorphism using a simple example: animals. Below is a UML[7] diagram describing a class structure:

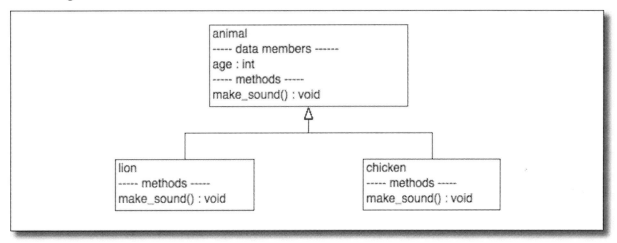

Figure 24: Animal UML Diagram

UML diagrams allow us to design and describe object-oriented class hierarchies in a visual way. In the case above, we have a ***base class*** called `animal` and two derived classes that extend the base class and describe animals: `lion` and `chicken`.

All animal classes have a data member, `age`, and one method: `make_sound()`. The `make_sound()` method prints the animal's sound to the screen.

---

[7] UML stands for Universal Modeling Language. In a way it is the schematic capture tool of object-oriented programming. More UML resources are available on www.uvmprimer.com.

Here is the code that implements the `animal` class:

```
1   class animal;
2       int age=-1;
3
4       function new(int a);
5           age = a;
6       endfunction : new
7
8       function void make_sound();
9           $fatal(1, "Generic animals don't have a sound.");
10      endfunction : make_sound
11
12  endclass : animal
13
```

Figure 25: The `animal` Class Code

The code above takes an animal's age as an argument and creates a new animal. The object has the `make_sound()` method, but this can't be used for a generic animal, so we return a fatal. If you try to create a generic animal and ask that generic animal to make a sound, the `$fatal` stops you.

Now we extend the `animal` class to create a `lion` class:

```
15  class lion extends animal;
16
17      function new(int age);
18          super.new(age);
19      endfunction : new
20
21      function void make_sound();
22          $display ("The Lion says Roar");
23      endfunction : make_sound
24
25  endclass : lion
```

Figure 26: The `lion` Class Code

The `lion` class extends `animal` and **inherits** the `age` data member from `animal`. The `new()` method passes `age` up to the `animal` constructor. It overrides the `make_sound()` method to make a lion sound.

The `chicken` code does the same things as the `lion` code, but with a different sound. The `new()` method in both classes call the super constructor and pass it the `age`.

This code raises a reasonable question: "If I'm just calling the `super.new()` constructor, why can't I simply inherit the constructor from my base class?" The answer is that our constructor has an argument and SystemVerilog requires that we explicitly write code for constructors that have arguments, even if they just call the super constructor.

Let's use these classes in a little program. We'll start with a conventional use model:

```
68      lion_h   = new(15);
69      lion_h.make_sound();
70      $display("The Lion is %0d years old", lion_h.age);
71
72      chicken_h = new(1);
73      chicken_h.make_sound();
74      $display("The Chicken is %0d years old", chicken_h.age);
75
```

Figure 27: Using the Animal Classes in a Conventional Way

Here we create a 15-year-old lion and a one-year-old chicken. We have them both make a sound.

The result looks like this:

```
24      # The Lion says Roar
25      # The Lion is 15 years old
26      # The Chicken says BECAWW
27      # The Chicken is 1 years old
```

Figure 28: Running the Lion and Chicken Code

This is good as far as it goes. We've created variables of type `lion` and `chicken,` filled them with objects, and the objects behave. But what if we create a variable called `animal_h` of type `animal`? Let's see what happens when we use that. Here is the code:

```
76      animal_h = lion_h;
77      animal_h.make_sound();
78      $display("The animal is %0d years old", animal_h.age);
79
80      animal_h = chicken_h;
81      animal_h.make_sound();
82      $display("The animal is %0d years old", animal_h.age);
83
```

Figure 29: Putting Lions and Chickens into the `animal_h` Variable

We've stored `lion` and `chicken` objects in the `animal_h` variable. This is legal because `lion` and `chicken` extends `animal`. Then we call the `make_sound()` method and get this result:

```
27      # The Chicken is 1 years old
28      # ** Fatal: Generic animals don't have a sound.
```

Figure 30: Fatal Error from Trying to Make the Animal Talk

This fatal error is happening because the `animal_h` variable is calling the `make_sound()` method defined in the `animal` class.

In a certain way, this makes sense. The variable is calling the method associated with its class. But in another way this does not make sense. The `animal_h` variable is holding a `lion` object.

In the real world you can put a lion into a box labeled "animal" and it will still be able to roar. So why can't we put a `lion` object in a variable of type `animal` and have it be able to roar?

It turns out that we can, but we have to tell SystemVerilog whether to use the function referenced by the variable type or by the object stored in that variable. We'll do that next.

virtual

Virtual Methods

SystemVerilog uses the keyword `virtual` in many places (overuses it, in my opinion). The keyword implies that the thing that is being defined as "virtual" is really a placeholder for something that will be provided later, or that is available in a different place.

When you declare a method to be a *virtual method,* you are telling SystemVerilog to ignore the superficial trappings of the variable type, and instead look deeper to the object stored within that variable. There you will find the true method.

Here is how you declare a virtual method:

```
1   class animal;
2       int age=-1;
3
4       function new(int a);
5           age = a;
6       endfunction : new
7
8       virtual function void make_sound();
9           $fatal(1, "Generic animals don't have a sound.");
10      endfunction : make_sound
11
12   endclass : animal
13
```

Figure 31: The `animal` Class with Virtual Functions

The only difference between the code above and the original animal code (Figure 25) is the keyword `virtual`.

The `make_sound()` method definitions in `lion` and `chicken` do not need the `virtual` keyword. They inherit this behavior from the base class, so their code does not change. Now our code in Figure 29 works as we expect:

```
25   # The Chicken says BECAWW
26   # The Chicken is 1 years old
27   # The Lion says Roar
28   # The animal is 15 years old
29   # The Chicken says BECAWW
30   # The animal is 1 years old
31
```

Figure 32: Running the Code with the Animal Variable

The `animal_h.makesound()` call returns different results based on the object stored in the animal variable.

Abstract Classes and Pure Virtual Functions

Our current version of the animal class provides a clunky solution to a simple problem. We want to force class users to override the `make_sound()` method, so we created a version of that method that calls `$fatal`. This means that our user will go all the way through the simulation and eventually hit a fatal error. In a big design this could take a half hour or more.

Wouldn't it be better if we could catch this error earlier? It turns out that we can.

SystemVerilog allows us to define a thing called an ***abstract class.*** Abstract classes can only be used as base classes. You cannot instantiate an object of an abstract class type. You will get a runtime error if you try.

When you define an abstract class, you can also define methods as ***pure virtual*** methods. These methods have no body and ***must*** be overridden when you override the base class. If you don't override them, you get a compilation error.

Abstract classes and pure virtual methods enforce discipline upon engineers who extend a base class. Pure virtual methods say, "You want to use my base class? That's fine. Here's the contract that describes what you have to do."

In our case, the `animal` class is a perfect candidate for an abstract class. There is no such thing as a generic animal.

Here is the abstract version of `animal`:

```
1   virtual class animal;
2       int age=-1;
3
4       function new(int a);
5           age = a;
6       endfunction : new
7
8       pure virtual function void make_sound();
9
10  endclass : animal
11
```

Figure 33: Virtual Animal Base Class

This is much simpler! We define the abstract class `animal`[8] and then pure virtual method `make_sound()`. We don't bother creating a body for `make_sound()`, because the overriding classes will handle that.

---

[8] Amazingly enough, the SystemVerilog definition team has found yet *another* slightly different way to use the keyword `virtual`.

Here's the new approach in action. First, let's try to instantiate an animal object directly:

```
46        animal animal_h;
47
48        animal_h = new(3);
49
50        lion_h  = new(15);
```

Figure 34: Trying to Instantiate a Virtual Class

The code works exactly the same way as before, but now we've introduced a way for SystemVerilog to catch errors. We try to instantiate an abstract animal above. Here's what happens:

```
22    # Loading work.top(fast)
23    # ** Fatal: (vsim-8250) Class allocator method 'new' called on Abstract Class.
24    #    Time: 0 ns  Iteration: 0  Process: /top/#INITIAL#42(#ublk#0#44) File: pure_virtual.sv
25    # Fatal error in Module top at pure_virtual.sv line 48
26    #
27    # HDL call sequence:
28    # Stopped at pure_virtual.sv 48 Module top
```

Figure 35: Bad Animal—No Biscuit for You

The Questa simulator correctly gave us a fatal runtime error when we tried to do the nonsensical thing of creating an abstract animal.

Summary of Polymorphism

In this chapter we examined the object-oriented trick of *polymorphism*. This will be a critical tool when we want to take advantage of the flexibility of the UVM.

In our next chapter, we'll learn how to create a library of common methods available to the entire testbench. We do this by defining a class that contains static variable and static method. This is another important tool that we'll use in the UVM.

Chapter 7

Static Methods and Variables

I despise global variables. Why? Partly because all the programming books tell me that I should despise global variables, but mostly because I've debugged global-variable-infested code. It's just terrible.

The first problem is that you can't easily find the type of a global variable. You go to the top of your function, and it's not declared there. You go to the top of the program, and it's not declared there. You finally have to do a search through all your source files to find the variable, and then you can see its type.

The second reason is that it's pretty easy for some other part of your program to change the value of a global variable without your expecting it. You store one number, but find another. These two reasons combined make me despise global variables.

That said, there are many cases, especially in testbench design, where it's useful to have a global data structure. For example, you might have one part of your testbench driving data into your DUT and another part reading results. You may want to store both halves of that transaction in a global location and have a third self-checking tool examine the results. This is a legitimate way to use global variables.

What we need is a way of using global storage that is easy to use and maintain. Object-oriented programming provides this functionality within class definitions using static variables and static methods. This makes it easy to define, use, and maintain global variables and global methods.

Declaring Static Variables

Back when we were discussing class definitions on page 35, I said that the memory that stored an object wasn't allocated until we called the `new()` method. It turns out this was only partially true. SystemVerilog behaves differently if we put a `static` keyword in front of a class's data member. If we do that, then the memory for that variable gets allocated as soon as we define the class.

Another aspect of static data members is that we have only one copy of them no matter how many times we instantiate the class to create new objects. All the objects see the same copy of the member. Essentially, we have created a global variable in a controlled way.

Let's go back to the lion example to see how to create static variables and use them. Let's say that we've decided to keep our lions in a cage. The "cage" in this case is a SystemVerilog queue that can store all our lions in an array and read them out later.

We can only have one cage for all the lions, so we can't create a cage variable in the `lion` class. Instead, we need to create a new class called `lion_cage` with a static variable that holds all our lions. The `lion_cage` class looks like this:

```
49
50    class lion_cage;
51
52        static lion cage[$];
53
54    endclass : lion_cage
55
```

Figure 36: The Lion's Cage

The `lion_cage` class contains one SystemVerilog queue defined as a static variable. The queue holds `lion` objects.

The `static` keyword in front of the declaration means that we can access the variable without instantiating an object of this class. This variable has only one copy, and that copy gets allocated as soon as we run the program. Now we can access the lion cage as many times as we want. Here is an example of us storing lions in the cage:

```
58        initial begin
59            lion    lion_h;
60            lion_h  = new(2,  "Kimba");
61            lion_cage::cage.push_back(lion_h);
62            lion_h  = new(3,  "Simba");
63            lion_cage::cage.push_back(lion_h);
64            lion_h  = new(15, "Mustafa");
65            lion_cage::cage.push_back(lion_h);
66            $display("Lions in cage");
67            foreach (lion_cage::cage[i])
68                $display(lion_cage::cage[i].get_name());
69        end
```

Figure 37: Putting Lions in a Cage

Here we're creating new lions[9] and then using our static variable to put them into the cage queue. Notice the `::` operator. We access the variable in the `lion_cage` class by naming the class and placing the `::` operator after its name. This tells the compiler that we want to access static variables inside the class's ***namespace***.

We access the cage with `lion_cage::cage` and use the `push_back()` method to store each lion in the queue.

The `foreach` operator allows us to access each location in the queue. Since each location contains a `lion` object, we use the `get_name()` method to print out the lion's name using the loop to step through the queue entries.

---

[9] The `lion` class has been modified to store the lion's name.

Here is the output:

```
23    # Lions in cage
24    # Kimba
25    # Simba
26    # Mustafa
27
```

Figure 38: An Inventory of Lions

This example showed how to create a global copy of a variable and access it from your code. The beauty of this system is that we can access the variable from everywhere and immediately see where the variable is declared. The class name comes before the :: operator, so if we want to modify the declaration we know to look in the class definition.

The problem is that accessing a raw static variable is poor coding style. It makes it more difficult for later engineers to know how to use our object because we've exposed the guts. For example, you might not know how to use SystemVerilog queues, and so you couldn't use the lion cage until you googled "SystemVerilog queues."

What we really want is a set of static methods that go along with our static variables. These methods hide our implementation and make it easier for future engineers to use our objects.

Declaring Static Methods

We've seen that we can successfully share a SystemVerilog queue globally by declaring the queue to be a static variable and letting users access the queue. But, we've decided that we want to hide the implementation of our lion cage from the user and instead give the user a programming interface to the cage. This will make it easier to use the object.

Here is the lion cage code that accomplishes this:

```
44    class lion_cage;
45
46        protected static lion cage[$];
47
48        static function void cage_lion(lion l);
49            cage.push_back(l);
50        endfunction : cage_lion
51
52        static function void list_lions();
53            $display("Lions in cage");
54            foreach (cage[i])
55                $display(cage[i].get_name());
56        endfunction : list_lions
57
58    endclass : lion_cage
```

Figure 39: The Lion Cage with Programming Interface

This new version of lion_cage is safer and easier to use than the previous version. First, we've protected our static variable with the protected keyword. This keyword enforces good reuse by preventing users from accessing our SystemVerilog queue directly. The SystemVerilog compiler will deliver a syntax error to any user who tries to access the cage variable directly. That way you can change the implementation in the future without breaking anyone else's code.

Instead of giving users access to our precious `cage` variable, we've provided them with two static access methods.

`cage_lion()` takes a `lion` object as an argument and stores said lion in the SystemVerilog queue.

`list_lions()` uses a SystemVerilog `foreach` loop to list out the lions.

The code that calls these methods is simpler than our previous code because it doesn't require the author to access the cage directly (never a safe thing to do when dealing with lions):

```
65    initial begin
66       lion    lion_h;
67       lion_h  = new(2,  "Kimba");
68       lion_cage::cage_lion(lion_h);
69       lion_h  = new(3,  "Simba");
70       lion_cage::cage_lion(lion_h);
71       lion_h  = new(15, "Mustafa");
72       lion_cage::cage_lion(lion_h);
73       lion_cage::list_lions();
74    end
```

Figure 40: Caging Lions Using Static Methods

In this code we create each of our lions and store him in the cage using the `lion_cage::cage_lion()` method. Then we list out all the lions with the `lion_cage::list_lions()` method.

All these calls to all these methods access the same memory location. We could also access the lion cage from anywhere in our program using the global reference to the `lion_cage` class.

Static Methods and Variables Summary

In this chapter we used static variables in class definitions to create global resources. We saw that SystemVerilog allows us to create global resources in a controlled way, and we learned how to define and access these global resources.

But our `lion_cage` class has a problem: it only works for lions. If we want to cage chickens as well, we'll have to copy this code and change the type of the static variable. This doesn't bode well for code reuse.

It turns out that SystemVerilog has solved this problem with parameterized class definitions. These are another crucial feature we need to understand to use the UVM, and so we'll examine parameterization next.

Chapter 8

Parameterized Class Definitions

In our last chapter, we created a class with static variables and definitions and used the class to cage lions. Our static class worked well and we were able to use a global resource in a logical way. However, we discovered a problem.

What if we want to make a chicken cage? When we look at the `lion_cage` code in Figure 39 we see that the `chicken_cage` class would look just like the `lion_cage` class except that we change the queue's type from `lion` to `chicken`.

The first instinct would be to copy the lion cage code and make a chicken cage. But that would be a mistake. A zoo that holds only a lion and a chicken is pretty lame. We'd certainly want to have other kinds of cages for other kinds of animals. Would we copy the code for all them?

We can imagine dozens of scenarios where we will want to make changes to cages in general (add a `feed()` method, for example.) If we copied the code, we'd have to make the changes in every copy. We'd be asking for bugs. This would get out of hand rapidly.

Fortunately, SystemVerilog has a feature that handles this problem: ***parameterized class definitions***. More importantly, the UVM uses parameterized classes extensively, so this is a language feature that we need to understand.

Let's create a parameterized class definition.

Making an Animal Cage

We all remember parameters from original Verilog.[10] Parameters are variables that we can set when we instantiate a module. The most famous example of parameters is a memory. We create a parameter for the data bus width and address bus width so that a user can reference the same module to instantiate a memory of any size. Here is an example:

```
1    module RAM #(awidth, dwidth) (
2                        input wire [awidth-1:0] address,
3                        inout wire [dwidth-1:0] data,
4                        input we);
5
6        initial $display("awidth: %0d  dwidth %0d",awidth, dwidth);
7        // code to implement RAM
8    endmodule // RAM
```

Figure 41: Parameters in a Module

---

[10] They are called generics in VHDL.

We're going to do the same thing to solve the cage problem, but instead of having the parameter be a number such as bus width, we're going to have it be a type. Here is the code for our generic animal cage:

```
60    class animal_cage #(type T);
61
62        protected static T cage[$];
63
64        static function void cage_animal(T l);
65            cage.push_back(l);
66        endfunction : cage_animal
67
68        static function void list_animals();
69            $display("Animals in cage:");
70            foreach (cage[i])
71                $display(cage[i].get_name());
72        endfunction : list_animals
73
74    endclass : animal_cage
```

Figure 42: Generic Animal Cage

The `animal_cage` code above is just like the `lion_cage` code except it has a parameter. We can see on the first line that we've defined a `type` parameter[11] called T, and then used that parameter to declare the type of the queue and as the argument type for `cage_animal`.

Now we can create different cage classes for each kind of animal using one code base. When we make edits here, they affect cages for all animals.

We use the cage by providing a type when we use the static methods:

```
81        initial begin
82            lion    lion_h;
83            chicken  chicken_h;
84            lion_h = new(15, "Mustafa");
85            animal_cage #(lion)::cage_animal(lion_h);
86            lion_h = new(15, "Simba");
87            animal_cage #(lion)::cage_animal(lion_h);
88
89            chicken_h = new(1, "Clucker");
90            animal_cage #(chicken)::cage_animal(chicken_h);
91            chicken_h = new(1, "Scratchy");
92            animal_cage #(chicken)::cage_animal(chicken_h);
93
94            $display("-- Lions --");
95            animal_cage #(lion)::list_animals();
96            $display("-- Chickens --");
97            animal_cage #(chicken)::list_animals();
98        end
```

Figure 43: Cages for Chickens and Lions

---

[11] Notice that T has no default. This forces the user to provide a value.

This example shows us how to access the static variables of our lion cages and chicken cages. We put the type of our animals after the # symbol and between the parentheses. For lions we access the `cage_animal` static method using the `lion` class as a parameter. For chickens we access the same method using `chicken` as the parameter.

The result is that we wind up with two copies of the static queue, one that stores lions and another that stores chickens. This highlights an important fact about parameterized classes. When you instantiate a parameterized class, you are creating a completely different version of that class with every different parameter. The `animal_cage #(lion)` class and the `animal_cage #(chicken)` class are completely different namespaces that happen to share source code.

We see this separation when we look at the output from the two calls to `list_animals()`:

```
23  # -- Lions --
24  # Animals in cage:
25  # Mustafa
26  # Simba
27  # -- Chickens --
28  # Animals in cage:
29  # Clucker
30  # Scratchy
31
```

Figure 44: Viewing Our Animals

You'll notice that we are not looking at one cage with four animals but at two cages with two animals each. The lions are kept separate from the chickens.

From reading this, you might get the impression that we can only use parameterized classes with static variables and methods. This is not the case. Let's look at another way of making our cages.

Declaring Variables with Parameters

While the UVM uses static methods and parameters, and even uses them together, the most common way we use parameterized types in the UVM is to declare variables. Let's modify our animal cage class to demonstrate.

In this example, we're no longer going to use static methods to access our animal cage. Instead we're going to instantiate an animal cage and use the object to store our other animals. Here is the new `animal_cage` code:

```
60   class animal_cage #(type T);
61
62       protected T cage[$];
63
64       function void cage_animal(T animal_h);
65           cage.push_back(animal_h);
66       endfunction : cage_animal
67
68       function void list_animals();
69           $display("Animals in cage:");
70           foreach (cage[i])
71               $display(cage[i].get_name());
72       endfunction : list_animals
73
74   endclass : animal_cage
75
```

Figure 45: Animal Cage: Ready for Instantiation

The only difference between the code above and the code in the previous section is that we've removed the keyword `static` from the variable and methods. We need to declare a variable that will hold this object and instantiate the object to use it.[12] We do that below.

```
78   module top;
79
80       lion    lion_h;
81       chicken chicken_h;
82
83       animal_cage #(lion)    lion_cage;
84       animal_cage #(chicken) chicken_cage;
85
86
```

Figure 46: Declaring the Cages

The code above is like the previous code, but now we have two new variables: `lion_cage` and `chicken_cage`. We declare these variables by passing the type of animal in the declaration. The compiler takes the type from the parameter and creates a new class using that parameter. Then it declares the variable. If you use a type that is incompatible with animal cage, say an object without the needed `get_name()` method you'll get a syntax error.

---

[12] You may have noticed that `animal_cage` has no explicit `new()` method. If you don't have any arguments in your constructor, SystemVerilog will provide a constructor for you.

Now we have variables that can hold animal objects and animal cage objects. Let's instantiate the variables using `new()` methods and be on our way:

```
87
88        initial begin
89            lion_cage = new();
90            lion_h = new(15, "Mustafa");
91            lion_cage.cage_animal(lion_h);
92            lion_h = new(15, "Simba");
93            lion_cage.cage_animal(lion_h);
94
95            chicken_cage = new();
96            chicken_h = new(1, "Little Red Hen");
97            chicken_cage.cage_animal(chicken_h);
98
99            chicken_h = new(1, "Lady Clucksalot");
100           chicken_cage.cage_animal(chicken_h);
101
102
103           $display("-- Lions --");
104           lion_cage.list_animals();
105           $display("-- Chickens --");
106           chicken_cage.list_animals();
107       end
```

Figure 47: Using the Animal Cages

The code above instantiates a new lion cage and then creates and cages two lions ("Mustafa" and "Simba"). Then it does the same thing for chickens. It creates a new `chicken_cage` and cages two chickens ("Little Red Hen" and "Lady Clucksalot"). Then we print out the animals:

```
23    # -- Lions --
24    # Animals in cage:
25    # Mustafa
26    # Simba
27    # -- Chickens --
28    # Animals in cage:
29    # Little Red Hen
30    # Lady Clucksalot
31
```

Figure 48: Looking at the Animals

The code works exactly the same way as the previous code. The big difference is that we cannot access the cages from just anywhere in the testbench. We create new cage objects and store the animals in them. When the task finishes, the objects go away.

Parameterized Class Definition Summary

In this chapter we learned about a SystemVerilog feature that is a cornerstone of the UVM: parameterized classes. This wraps up our overview of object-oriented programming features in SystemVerilog.

In our next chapter, we're going to put several of these object-oriented features together to implement a class called a factory. We're doing this because the factory pattern is a key part of the UVM, and it would behoove us to understand how it works.

Plus, it's neat.

Chapter 9

The Factory Pattern

In some ways object-oriented programming reminds me of chess. We learn chess as a two-step process. First we learn the moves: the knight moves like this, the queen moves like that, the pawn can capture *en passant*. Then we learn how to use those moves to create combinations: the nasty pin, the terrifying knight fork, and the devastating discovered check.

We're learning object-oriented programming the same way. We've learned about the moves: class extension, polymorphism, static methods, and parameterized classes. Now we'll learn some combinations and programming tricks.

Object-oriented programming engineers like to create new words. They've replaced the phrase *programming tricks* with the much classier phrase *design patterns*. Like the "pin" and the "knight fork," these design patterns form a vocabulary that object-oriented programmers use to describe the architecture of their solutions. We're going to look at *the factory pattern*.

The factory is the most visible design pattern in the UVM. We'll see later how we use it to create dynamically adaptable testbenches. Since it is used so extensively, we'll create a simple factory in this chapter to show how the pattern works.

Why Use the Factory Pattern?

The factory pattern addresses a limitation in the way we've been instantiating our objects until this point. Consider the way we instantiated the objects in our previous example:

```
90      lion_h = new(15, "Mustafa");
91      lion_cage.cage_animal(lion_h);
92      lion_h = new(15, "Simba");
93      lion_cage.cage_animal(lion_h);
94
95      chicken_cage = new();
96      chicken_h = new(1, "Little Red Hen");
97      chicken_cage.cage_animal(chicken_h);
98
99      chicken_h = new(1, "Lady Clucksalot");
00      chicken_cage.cage_animal(chicken_h);
```

Figure 49: Instantiating Objects by Calling the `new()` Method

As you can see, we've made calls to `new()` in order to create all our objects. These calls are written into our source code. If we want to create a different set of objects, or even add new kinds of animals, we need to modify our source code. This is a severe limitation.

We call this *hardcoding*. So you might say, "I see that you're hardcoding those animal instantiations, Ray. What if I want to change the animals?"

That's a good question.

Consider a case where we want to read a list of animals from a file and instantiate objects to represent them. This is a dynamic way of choosing our animals, and it's nearly impossible to accomplish with hardcoded instantiations. We'd have to run the file through a script that turned it into source code, compile the source code, and then run our program. We'd have to recompile our program every time we changed our data. This is bad—very bad.

It gets worse if we want to write a program that dynamically generates the data. For example, say we wanted to randomly choose our animals, or balance the numbers of animals based on other animals. We cannot do any of these things if we're hardcoding our constructors.

The factory pattern solves this problem.

Creating an Animal Factory

In the factory pattern we want to pass an argument to a method and receive back an object of the type we specify. In our simple example, we're going to use a string as the argument.[13] We're going to create a factory that generates animals. Before we do that, let's remember our animal class hierarchy:

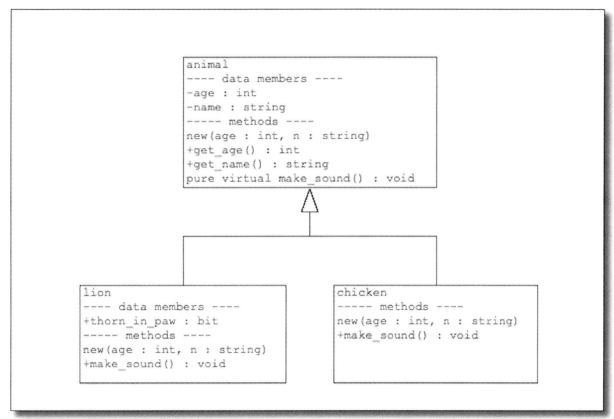

Figure 50: The Animal Class Hierarchy[14]

We see here that the `lion` class and the `chicken` class both extend the `animal` class, and we remember from our chapter on polymorphism that the `chicken` and lion `classes` override the pure virtual method, `makesound()` and the construtor `new()`. These are their only differences from the base class.

---

[13] The UVM has a much more clever approach than this, but it's beyond the scope of this book to talk about how that works.

[14] The + and − signs in this diagram tell us whether a member is protected. The + means that the member is public, the − means it's protected. For example, `thorn_in_paw` is public.

Since we can store any kind of animal in an `animal` variable, we can also create a function that returns any kind of animal as an `animal` variable. We'll use this fact to create our factory:

```
50   class animal_factory;
51
52       static function animal make_animal(string species,
53                                           int age, string name);
54           chicken chicken;
55           lion lion;
56           case (species)
57             "lion" : begin
58               lion = new(age, name);
```

Figure 51: Declaring Our Animal Factory

We've created a new class called `animal_factory`. The class contains one static method `make_animal`. The `make_animal` method takes a species name as a string along with the age and name of the animal. It will make an animal of that species and return it as an `animal`.

The `make_animal` method contains two variables of type `chicken` and `lion`. We'll use these to call our constructor and get the correct type of animal, as we see below:

```
54           chicken chicken;
55           lion lion;
56           case (species)
57             "lion" : begin
58               lion = new(age, name);
59               return lion;
60             end
61
62             "chicken" : begin
63               chicken = new(age, name);
64               return chicken;
65             end
66
67             default :
68               $fatal (1, {"No such animal: ", species});
69
70           endcase // case (species)
```

Figure 52: Making New Animals

The key to our factory is the `case` statement. The case statement looks at the `species` string and creates the correct animal (and fatals out if no such animal exists). Since the function returns an `animal`, we are allowed to return either a `lion` or a `chicken` object.

We now have an animal factory and can dynamically create different kinds of animals.

Using the Animal Factory

Since `animal_factory` has a static method, we can use it from anywhere in the testbench. We'll test our factory using an `initial` block:

```
99    initial begin
100       animal animal_h;
101       lion    lion_h;
102       chicken  chicken_h;
103
104       animal_h =
105              animal_factory::make_animal("lion", 15, "Mustafa");
106       animal_h.make_sound();
107       if (animal_h.thorn_in_paw) $display("He looks angry!");
```

Figure 53: Making an Animal

We've declared three variables: `animal_h`, `lion_h`, and `chicken_h`.

We call the `make_animal()` method in our factory and tell it that we want a lion named Mustafa who's 15 years old. The factory creates a lion and stores him in `animal_h` using polymorphism. Let's take a moment to use some of the features of polymorphism.

First we call the `make_sound()` method on the `animal_h` variable. This works because we've declared `make_sound()` to be a virtual method. The simulator will call the method defined in the `lion` class because there is a lion stored in the `animal_h` variable.

However, we learn the limits of polymorphism when we try to use the `thorn_in_paw` data member from the `lion` class. The compiler correctly gives us the following error:

```
5    # ** Error: factory.sv(107): Field/method name (thorn_in_paw) not in 'animal_h'
6    # ** Error: /tools/mentor/questa/10.1c_1/questasim/linux/vlog failed.
```

Figure 54: Syntax Error When Trying to Access `thorn_in_paw` Using the `animal_h` Object

The compiler error clearly explains the problem. We defined the `thorn_in_paw` variable in the `lion` class, not the `animal` class (see Figure 50), so the compiler is correct to complain. We can access the `make_sound()` method because it's defined in both.

If we want to access `lion`-only data members, we need to convert our animal object into a lion object. This is called *casting* the animal as a lion. We cast a variable like this:

```
105       animal_h =
106            animal_factory::make_animal("lion", 15, "Mustafa");
107       animal_h.make_sound();
108
109       cast_ok = $cast(lion_h, animal_h);
110       if ( ! cast_ok)
111          $fatal(1, "Failed to cast animal_h to lion_h");
```

Figure 55: Casting the `factory_result` into the `lion` Variable

The $cast system call tells the simulator that we want to convert the variable in the second argument (animal_h of type animal) into the class of the first argument (lion_h of type lion), and copy at the same time. This only works if the target class is a child of the casted class. You cannot cast lion into chicken.

The $cast system call returns a 1'b1 if the cast is successful and a 1'b0 if the cast fails. It's important for your sanity that you check this every time you cast a variable. In this example, I stored the status in the variable cast_ok and then checked it, but you can combine these steps into one statement as below.

We can combine casting with a call to the factory and an error check to return exactly the type of animal we want:

```
115
116    if (!$cast(lion_h, animal_factory::make_animal("lion", 2, "Simba")))
117       $fatal(1, "Failed to cast animal from factory to lion_h");
118
119    animal_cage#(lion)::cage_animal(lion_h);
120
121    if(!$cast(chicken_h ,animal_factory::make_animal("chicken", 1, "Clucker")))
122       $fatal(1, "Failed to cast animal factory result to chicken_h");
123
124    animal_cage #(chicken)::cage_animal(chicken_h);
125
```

Figure 56: Casting Our Animal into the Appropriate Variable

We've successfully created a factory for our animals!

Factory Pattern Summary

In this example of the factory, we learned how to dynamically create different types of objects without modifying our source code. It is true that in this case we hardcoded the strings for the calls to the factory ("lion," "chicken") but we could have just as easily have read them from a file.

When we start building testbenches with the UVM, we'll use the factory to dynamically create our testbench components. We'll also learn that the UVM factory allows us to override objects so that you might ask for a generic "lion," but instead you'll get an "eastern mountain lion."

We have all the concepts we need to start creating testbenches using object-oriented code. Let's go back to the TinyALU and get started.

Chapter 10

An Object-Oriented Testbench

And now, the moment we've been waiting for: the creation of an object-oriented testbench (cue lightning, thunder, and maniacal laughter).

The very creation of this testbench raises a fair question: Why bother? Why go through the process of learning object-oriented programming and then using that paradigm to create a testbench? Weren't the old ways good enough?

Simple answer: No.

We've shown here that traditional Verilog programming is good enough to validate a simple design such as the TinyALU. It would even be good enough to validate a more complex design, such as a Wishbone to I2C block. The impossibility arrives when you start trying to verify more complex designs, such as Ethernet switches with hundreds of ports, or CPUs with three levels of cache.

At that point you need to implement complex predictors, extensive coverage tools, and robust stimulus generators. You need them to scale from unit test to system test, and you need a large team of engineers to work together with a common framework. Finally, you also need to make all this reusable because it's too much work to write one of these testbenches from scratch for every project.

Object-oriented programming, with its clearly encapsulated behavior, enforced rules of reuse, and nifty memory management approach, is the only programming technology that can handle all this complexity.

The TinyALU Testbench in Objects

As we work through *The UVM Primer*, we are going to take the simple TinyALU testbench and transform it into a complete UVM testbench. This allows us to look at each of the concepts in the UVM using a concrete example.

Our first step is to convert the module-based testbench that we created in Chapter 3 into an object-based testbench. Our first object-oriented testbench will contain one module and four classes:

- `top`—The top-level module that instantiates the `testbench` class

- `testbench`—The top-level class

- `tester`—Drives stimulus

- `scoreboard`—Checks that the TinyALU is working

- `coverage`—Captures functional coverage information

These classes will change over the course of the book as we introduce more features of the UVM, but their basic roles will remain unchanged. Let's start by looking at the top-level module.

The Object-Based Top-Level Module

In our module-based testbench, we connected the modules using a SystemVerilog interface. We do the same thing when we create an object-oriented testbench. Each class gets a copy of the interface so it can manipulate signals.

Our top-level testbench does three things:

- Imports the class definitions

- Instantiates the DUT and BFM and declares the testbench class variable

- Instantiates and launches the testbench class

These three basic tasks exist in all object-oriented testbenches, though different testbenches accomplish this different ways. Let's walk through the top-level module.

Import the Class Definitions

When we create an object-oriented testbench, we store all the class definitions and shared resources in SystemVerilog packages. Packages allow us to share class and variable definitions across multiple modules. When you import a package, you get access to everything defined or declared in that package.

Our package is called the `tinyalu_pkg`. It defines all our classes. We get access to those definitions by importing the package into our module:

```
1    module top;
2      import   tinyalu_pkg::*;
3    `include "tinyalu_macros.svh"
4
5        tinyalu DUT ( .A(bfm.A), .B(bfm.B), .op(bfm.op),
```

Figure 57: Importing the `tinyalu_pkg` and Including the TinyALU Macros

The `tinyalu_pkg` defines the four classes in the testbench and the `tinyalu_macros.svh` file defines useful macros. As we'll see later, the UVM also uses this package/macro one-two punch to deliver its functionality.

Instantiate the DUT and BFM; Declare the Testbench Class Variable

We've defined the testbench variable in the package. In the top-level module, we instantiate the DUT and the BFM while declaring a variable to hold our testbench:

```
5    tinyalu DUT (.A(bfm.A), .B(bfm.B), .op(bfm.op),
6                 .clk(bfm.clk), .reset_n(bfm.reset_n),
7                 .start(bfm.start), .done(bfm.done), .result(bfm.result));
8
9    tinyalu_bfm    bfm();  ← contains all signal-level behavior
10
11   testbench      testbench_h;
12
```

Figure 58: Instantiating the DUT and BFM while Declaring the Class Variable

The code above is similar to our module-based code, except that we've replaced the stimulus, self-check, and coverage modules with the `testbench` class. We've declared a variable `testbench_h` that will store our `testbench` object.

Instantiate and Launch the `testbench` Object

Now we need to instantiate the testbench object and pass it a handle to the BFM. Once we've done that, we launch a method in `testbench_h` that verifies the TinyALU:

```
13
14       initial begin
15           testbench_h = new(bfm);
16           testbench_h.execute();
17       end
18
19   endmodule : top
```

Figure 59: Instantiating and Launching the Testbench

We create a new testbench and pass it a handle to the BFM as an argument to `new()`. This is similar to instantiating a module and placing the BFM on the port list. Then we call the `testbench_h.execute()` method to verify the TinyALU.

Because the testbench object has a copy of the BFM, it can use the tasks in the BFM to drive stimulus and can watch the signals to check output and coverage.

Next, let's dig in and look at the classes in the testbench.

The `testbench` Class

Object-oriented testbenches have a single object at the top of the testbench that instantiates other objects, connects them together and launches their methods. We'll see in the next chapter that the UVM handles many of these functions for us, but since we're not using the UVM yet, we need to do all this work ourselves. The `testbench` class does that work.

Declarations

The `testbench` class is the top level of the testbench hierarchy. It declares variables to hold the other parts of the testbench, instantiates those objects, and launches them. First we need to handle the declarations. When we do this, we'll learn about a new use for the ubiquitous keyword `virtual`.

```
1   class testbench;
2
3       virtual tinyalu_bfm bfm;
4
5       tester     tester_h;
6       coverage   coverage_h;
7       scoreboard scoreboard_h;
8
9       function new (virtual tinyalu_bfm b);
10          bfm = b;
11      endfunction : new
12
```

Figure 60: Declarations and Construction

The `testbench` class definition above contains a mysterious declaration: "`virtual tinyalu_bfm bfm.`" What is this `virtual tinyalu_bfm` thing?

It's the object world's equivalent of a module's port list.

We saw back in our module-based code example that the SystemVerilog interface is a single compiled unit that delivers all the signals in the testbench to modules. The `tester`, `scoreboard`, and `coverage` modules got a copy of the BFM through their module port list.

Objects can access signals the same way, by getting a handle to a SystemVerilog interface. The `virtual` declaration tells the compiler that this variable will be given a handle to an interface sometime in the future. The keyword `virtual` acknowledges that the interface handle isn't in `bfm` variable at compile time, but will be there by the time someone tries to access the signals.

There are lots of ways to get a handle to the interface into the `bfm` variables. In this case, we provide the `bfm` the `new()` method. Later versions of this class will use other approaches.

An object-oriented testbench uses classes and objects, rather than modules, to verify the DUT. We declare three variables (`tester_h`, `coverage_h`, and `scoreboard_h`) to hold the three testbench objects.

The `execute()` Method

Now that we've declared variables for the tester, coverage collector, and scoreboard, we need to instantiate these objects and launch them. We do all our verification using a task called `execute()`. This is the task that we launched in the initial block of the top-level module (Figure 59.)

The execute() task instantiates the testbench objects, then launches their execute() methods:

```
13      task execute();
14          tester_h      = new(bfm);
15          coverage_h    = new(bfm);
16          scoreboard_h = new(bfm);
17
18          fork
19              tester_h.execute();
20              coverage_h.execute();
21              scoreboard_h.execute();
22          join_none
23      endtask : execute
24  endclass : testbench
25
```

Figure 61: Launching the Testbench Objects

The execute() method instantiates the three testbench objects, passing each one a copy of the bfm. Then it launches the execute() methods inside the objects using the fork/join_none construct to create three threads, one for each testbench component. This is the same thing as instantiating three modules, each with its own initial or always block.

The top-level execute() method exits after launching the threads, but the threads live on, simulating the DUT.

Let's look at each of these objects. They are equivalent to their module counterparts, but have some minor changes to make them into classes.

The tester Class

The tester stimulates the TinyALU with random operations that eventually cover all the functional coverpoints. The class-based tester is identical to the module-based tester (Figure 16), with three differences: we define a class instead of a module, we use a variable to access the BFM rather than a port list, and we use the execute() method rather than an initial block.

Here is the class declaration and the variable that holds the BFM:

```
1   class tester;
2
3       virtual tinyalu_bfm bfm;
4
5       function new (virtual tinyalu_bfm b);
6           bfm = b;
7       endfunction : new
8
```

Figure 62: The tester Definition

The code above defines the class called tester, declares a variable to hold the BFM, and loads that variable in the constructor.

Now we create an `execute()` method. We rely upon the top-level class to call this method:

```
36    task execute();
37        byte        unsigned        iA;
38        byte        unsigned        iB;
39        shortint    unsigned        result;
40        operation_t                 op_set;
41        bfm.reset_alu();
42        op_set = rst_op;
43        iA = get_data();
44        iB = get_data();
```

Figure 63: The `execute()` Method

The `execute()` task is identical to the `initial` block from the original module. It generates 1000 randomized transactions then calls `$stop` to end the simulation.

The `scoreboard` Class

The `scoreboard` class is almost identical to the module. The only difference is the `class` keyword and the way we get the `bfm` into the object rather than into the module.

```
1    class scoreboard;
2        virtual tinyalu_bfm bfm;
3
4      function new (virtual tinyalu_bfm b);
5        bfm = b;
6      endfunction : new
7
8      task execute();
9        shortint predicted_result;
10       forever begin : self_checker
11           @(posedge bfm.done)
12               case (bfm.op_set)
13                   add_op: predicted_result = bfm.A + bfm.B;
```

Figure 64: The `scoreboard` Class

The scoreboard in the module (Figure 15) uses an `always` block with the positive edge of `done` in its sensitivity list. We recreate that in our `execute()` method with a `forever` loop and an event statement that waits on the positive edge of the clock.

The rest of the code is the same as the module.

The `coverage` Class

The `coverage` class is just like the module in that we define two covergroups and sample them. The only difference lies in the way one does this in a class vs. the original module.

In the module, we defined the covergroups, then declared variables that held the covergroups, treating the covergroups as types. The variable declaration caused the covergroup to be created, and we could call the `sample()` method on the variable.

In a class, we don't need to declare variables to hold the covergroups, but we do need to call a constructor to create them. Behold:

```
81
82      function new (virtual interface tinyalu_bfm b);
83        op_cov = new();
84        zeros_or_ones_on_ops = new();
85        bfm = b;
86      endfunction : new
87
```

Figure 65: The `coverage` Constructor

The constructor handles the BFM the same way as the other constructors. It also instantiates the `op_cov` covergroup and the `zeros_or_ones_on_ops` covergroup using the `new()` keyword.

Putting It Together

We now see how the whole object-oriented testbench works. The top-level module instantiates a DUT and SystemVerilog interface as a BFM. It connects the DUT to the BFM in the instantiation (Figure 58).

The top-level `initial` block creates a top-level testbench object and passes a handle to the BFM to the object as the argument to the `new()` method. The top-level testbench class creates verification objects and passes each of them a copy of the BFM's handle (Figure 61).

Once the top-level object has created the verification objects, it launches their `execute()` methods using a `fork/join_none` block to give each object its own thread (Figure 61). Our testbench runs as it did with modules. The difference is that we have the flexibility and reuse power of object-oriented programming.

Object-Oriented Testbench Summary

In this chapter we learned how to create a simple testbench using objects instead of modules. We saw that the top-level module has to declare the objects in the testbench, instantiate them, and then launch them all in their own threads.

We are ready to start using the UVM. As we work through the rest of the book, we'll build upon the basic idea in this chapter to create more and more powerful versions of this simple object-oriented testbench.

This is what we've been waiting for. Let's get started by learning about UVM Tests.

Chapter 11

UVM Tests

We now know enough about testbench design, SystemVerilog interfaces, and object-oriented programming to start creating testbenches with the UVM. We'll start by understanding UVM Tests.

Verification teams need to be able to run thousands of tests on a design without recompiling their testbench for each test. Consider the case where a team is running 1,000 tests and takes 5 minutes per test to compile the testbench. That's 5,000 minutes, or 3.5 days of compilation time. That means you would literally spend half a week compiling the design.

We need to be able to compile the whole testbench once and then run it with different arguments to create the thousands of tests.

The UVM allows you to implement this dynamically configurable testbench. It allows you to create a testbench by defining object classes and then instantiating different objects for different tests.

The TinyALU testbench from the last chapter is almost entirely hardcoded. If we want to run a test with different stimulus from the random stimulus in our tester, we need to rewrite the tester object and recompile it.

We are going to learn about the UVM by turning the hardcoded TinyALU testbench into a dynamic testbench one step at a time.

Let's start with the problem of running multiple tests with one compilation.

Creating Tests with the Factory

Back in chapter 9, we discussed the factory pattern. This is an object-oriented programming trick that allows us to dynamically create objects based on data (such as a string) that is available at run time.

We learned about the factory pattern because it is a critical aspect of the UVM. The UVM allows you to use its factory to build almost anything, and this allows you to create dynamically adaptable testbenches.

In this case, we're going to ask the UVM to use its factory to launch different tests. We want to be able to run commands such as these:

```
31   vsim testbench -coverage +UVM_TESTNAME=add_test
32   vsim testbench -coverage +UVM_TESTNAME=random_test
```

Figure 66: Invoking Multiple Tests with One Compile

In the above example we compiled the testbench once, then ran different tests on it by supplying different test names at run time. The testbench was able to interpret these names and launch different tests based upon them.

We implemented this using the UVM by defining two classes: `add_test` and `random_test`. The UVM is using the `UVM_TESTNAME` string to call its factory and create instances of these classes. Once the UVM has instantiated the correct class, it launches the simulation.

Launching Simulations with the UVM

It's all well and good to wave our hands and say, "The UVM reads the `+UVM_TESTNAME` parameter, creates the object, and runs the simulation." But we can't actually write code with that broad description. We need to know how the UVM does its job so we can write classes that fit with it. We also need to know how to start tests using the UVM.

As we work with the UVM, we'll see that it handles most of the mundane tasks associated with simulating a testbench. For example, any object-oriented testbench needs to instantiate the equivalent of the top-level `testbench` class, so the UVM automates that step for us. We'll also see that it automates the process of instantiating objects within the `testbench` class and launching them in their own threads.

For now, we'll just see how the UVM automatically creates the equivalent of the top-level `testbench` object.

In the object-oriented testbench from the previous chapter we simulated a SystemVerilog module that instantiated the top-level class (`testbench`), then launched the test by calling the `testbench_h.execute()` method. The UVM does these things for us.

In our new module, we do two things: store a handle to the BFM and call the `run_test()` method:

```
1   module top;
2       import uvm_pkg::*;
3   `include "uvm_macros.svh"
4
5       import    tinyalu_pkg::*;
6   `include "tinyalu_macros.svh"
7
8       tinyalu_bfm        bfm();
9       tinyalu DUT (.A(bfm.A), .B(bfm.B), .op(bfm.op),
10               .clk(bfm.clk), .reset_n(bfm.reset_n),
11               .start(bfm.start), .done(bfm.done), .result(bfm.result));
12
13      initial begin
14          uvm_config_db #(virtual interface tinyalu_bfm)::set(null, "*", "bfm", bfm);
15          run_test();
16      end
17
18      endmodule : top
```

Figure 67: Top-Level Module Using the UVM

The top-level module demonstrates a typical pattern of using the UVM. First we import the `uvm_pkg` and its associated macros; these contain all the UVM class definitions, methods, and objects. Next we import the `tinyalu_pkg` and its associated macros; these contain *our* class definitions and a variable that holds the BFM. Then we include our macros and the UVM macros.

This package/macro combination is typical for testbenches across the industry.

We instantiate the BFM and DUT as we did before.

The `initial` block that launches the test is different from the one in our previous module (Figure 59). The first thing to notice is the way we pass the BFM handle to our objects.

In our previous example, we passed the BFM handle to our objects through the constructor. We can't do that with this testbench because the UVM needs specific arguments in the constructor. Instead we use a feature of the UVM: the `uvm_config_db` class.

The UVM developers used static classes and parameterization to make it easy to store global information across the testbench in an organized way. This system works the same way as the animal cage class in Figure 43, but instead of calling `cage_animal` we are calling `set`.

The first two arguments to `set` are `null` and `"*"`. They tell `set` to make the data available across the entire testbench. The third argument is a string that names the data we're storing in the database, the fourth argument is the value being stored, in this case the handle to the `tinyalu_bfm`.

Once we've stored the BFM in a global location, we can start the test. The `uvm_pkg` we imported at the top of the file defines the `run_test()` task. We start the test by calling `run_test()`.

The `run_test()` task reads the +UVM_TESTNAME parameter from the simulation's command line and instantiates an object of that class name. We can avoid using +UVM_TESTNAME by passing `run_test()` a string that contains the test name, but of course this defeats the whole idea of being able to launch many tests with one compile.

We've now achieved the first step in creating a testbench that can run multiple tests with one compile. The `run_test()` method above gets a string from the command line and uses the UVM factory to create a test object of that class. The test object gets the test rolling.

We have to define the `random_test` and `add_test` classes for this scheme to work. Let's do that next.

Defining and Registering a UVM Test

We saw above that the UVM uses its factory and a string on the command line to create a top-level test object and launch it. We need to define the test classes for this to work. Let's start by defining the `random_test` class:

```
1   class random_test extends uvm_test;
2     `uvm_component_utils(random_test);
3
4   virtual interface tinyalu_bfm bfm;
5
6   function new (string name, uvm_component parent);
7     super.new(name,parent);
8     if(!uvm_config_db #(virtual interface tinyalu_bfm)::get(null, "*","bfm", bfm))
9       $fatal("Failed to get BFM");
10  endfunction : new
11
12
```

Figure 68: The Top of the `random_test` Class

The first thing to notice is that `random_test` extends a class called `uvm_test`. The `uvm_test` class extends a class called `uvm_component` and so `random_test` is also an extension of `uvm_component`.

In order to extend `uvm_component` we need to follow strict rules when we write the mandatory `new()` method:

- The constructor must have two arguments called name and parent that are defined in that order: name is the first argument, parent is the second argument.

- The name argument must be of type string. The parent argument must be of type `uvm_component`.

- The constructor's first executable line must call `super.new(name, parent)`. The UVM will only work properly if you make this call.

Once we've fulfilled our obligations to our parent class, we can do whatever we like in the rest of the constructor. We call `uvm_config_db`'s `get()` method to get a handle to the `bfm`. Notice that we pass the `"bfm"` string that we used in `set()` and a variable that will hold the BFM. The `get()` method returns a 0 if the retrieval failed. We test for the status bit and fatal out of the simulation on a failure.

We have to do one last thing to define our class: we need to register it with the factory. If you look back at our animal factory (Figure 52) you'll see that it hardcodes the kinds of animals the factory can handle. We could only add an animal to the factory by modifying the factory's source code.

The UVM developers did not want us to have to modify their source code, so they created a mechanism to solve the problem and delivered it in the `uvm_component_utils` macro. We use that macro right after the `class` statement. The macro registers our `random_test` class with the factory. Now the factory can create `random_test` objects.[15]

The `run_phase()` Method

If you go back and look at the object-oriented chapter, you'll see that the module instantiates the top-level test object then launches it by calling `tb.execute()`. The UVM does something similar. When we call `run_test()` in the top-level module, the UVM creates a test object using the factory and launches the test object by calling the `run_phase()` method. The UVM defines `uvm_test` as having a `run_phase()` method and it uses `run_phase()` to execute our test.

We must override the `run_phase()` method to get our test to do anything. The task definition must be called `run_phase()` and it must have a single argument of type `uvm_phase` called `phase`. Here is our `run_phase()` definition:

```
12
13      task run_phase(uvm_phase phase);
14          random_tester    random_tester_h;
15          coverage   coverage_h;
16          scoreboard scoreboard_h;
17
18          phase.raise_objection(this);
19
20          random_tester_h    = new(bfm);
21          coverage_h  = new(bfm);
22          scoreboard_h = new(bfm);
23
24          fork
25              coverage_h.execute();
26              scoreboard_h.execute();
27          join_none
28
29          random_tester_h.execute();
30          phase.drop_objection(this);
31      endtask : run_phase
32
33  endclass
```

Figure 69: The `run_phase()` Method

The UVM calls the `run_phase()` method after it creates our object. This code is similar to the code in our object-oriented example. We've added two lines to tell our testbench when it can stop. We do this by *raising an objection*.

_____

[15] We'll see later that there is also a `` `uvm_object_utils() `` for classes that are not `uvm_components`.

Hey, I'm Working Here! Understanding Objections

It's easier to start a testbench than to stop it. You start a testbench with a simple call to `run_test()`, but that call can spawn hundreds of objects, each running in its own thread. Some testbenches will have several objects providing stimulus from different ports, and all those objects need to finish before you can end the test.

How do you know when to stop the test?

One kludgey solution to this problem is simply to run the testbench for some long period of time and assume that all the objects will get their work done within that time. This is a poor solution because at best it wastes time and at worst you run out of time before you've completed your stimulus.

If you think about it, the testbench problem of when to finish the test is similar to the office problem of when to turn off the lights. If we leave the lights on we waste electricity, but if we turn them off when people are in the room they get angry. We solve the problem by turning the lights off unless somebody objects. (Many offices implement this solution with a motion sensor.)

The UVM solves its finishing problem the same way. The test runs as long as some object in the testbench objects to finishing it. UVM objects have the ability to *raise an objection* to finishing the test. The test runs as long as one object has an objection to stopping it.

As the developer, you need to raise an objection before you start generating your stimulus and drop the objection when you're done. At that point you're telling the UVM, "It's fine with me if you finish the test." The test stops when all the objects have dropped their objections.

We said above that the `run_phase()` method must have a single argument of type `uvm_phase` called `phase`. We use the `phase` object to raise and drop objections.

We raise an objection by calling the `phase.raise_objection()` method and passing it a handle to ourselves (the `this` keyword always holds that handle in object-oriented programming). We now know that the test will run until we drop the objection.

After we call `raise_objection()` we instantiate our testbench objects, launch the `coverage_h.execute()` and `scoreboard_h.execute()` methods in their own threads, then call `tester.execute()`.

When `tester_h.execute()` returns we are done with the test, so we call the `phase.drop_objection()` method. The simulation ends at that point because there are no raised objections.

Writing the `add_test` Class

We started this example with the goal of launching multiple tests (Figure 66) without having to recompile our testbench. We created the `random_test` class as our first test. Now we need to create the `add_test` class.

The `add_test` class is almost identical to the `random_test` class except for a different tester object:

```
1   class add_test extends uvm_test;
2     `uvm_component_utils(add_test);
3
4       virtual interface tinyalu_bfm bfm;
5
6     function new (string name, uvm_component parent);
7       super.new(name,parent);
8       if(!uvm_config_db #(virtual interface tinyalu_bfm)::get(null, "*","bfm", bfm))
9         $fatal("Failed to get BFM");
10    endfunction : new
11
12
13      task run_phase(uvm_phase phase);
14        add_tester   add_tester_h;
15        coverage  coverage h;
```

Figure 70: The `add_test` Class

As you can see on lines 1 and 2, we create the `add_test` class by extending `uvm_test` and then we register `add_test` with the factory using the `` `uvm_component_utils() `` macro.

The only difference between `random_test` and `add_test` is the class of the tester object. Our new tester object is an instance of the `add_tester` class rather than `tester`.

Now we can run our two tests:

```
1     # vsim +UVM_TESTNAME=random_test top
2     ...
3     # UVM_INFO @ 0: reporter [RNTST] Running test random_test...
4     ...
5     # vsim +UVM_TESTNAME=add_test top
6     ...
7     # UVM_INFO @ 0: reporter [RNTST] Running test add_test...
8
```

Figure 71: Voila! Running Two Tests with One Compilation

UVM Test Summary

In this chapter we used the UVM for the first time. We defined top-level classes as extensions of `uvm_test` and used these classes to start multiple tests from one compilation.

The tests we created in this chapter instantiated testbench objects such as `scoreboard` and launched those objects in their own threads. This notion of instantiating objects inside of other objects to create a test is called ***creating a testbench hierarchy***. The UVM supports creating a testbench hierarchy using a class called `uvm_component`. We'll examine that class in the next chapter when we convert our testbench classes into extensions of `uvm_component`.

Chapter 12

UVM Components

Testbench design can be broken down into three pieces: structure, sequences, and data. The structure describes the testbench's pieces and how they fit together. The sequences describe the commands we send to our DUT and in what order, and the data describes the stimulus data we use in the commands.

We're going to spend the next few chapters talking about creating testbench structure using the UVM. The UVM describes a testbench using a hierarchy of objects. It gives us tools to consistently instantiate, launch, and terminate all the objects in our testbench design.

The `uvm_component` class is the foundation of testbench structure. For example, the `uvm_test` that we extended in our previous chapter is a `uvm_component`. Later we will use classes such as `uvm_subscriber` and `uvm_driver` that also extend `uvm_component`.

To do anything with the UVM, you need to be comfortable defining and instantiating UVM components. Here is a checklist:

- Step 1: Extend the `uvm_component` class or child class to define your component.
- Step 2: Use the `uvm_component_utils()` macro to register this class with the factory.
- Step 3: Provide at least the minimum `uvm_component` constructor.
- Step 4: Override the UVM phase methods (described below) as necessary.

In the previous chapter, we extended `uvm_test` and instantiated the three pieces of our testbench as generic objects. In this chapter we'll recast the tester, coverage, and scoreboard classes as `uvm_components` and instantiate them in the test using standard UVM practice.

Let's recast the `scoreboard` class as a `uvm_component` using these steps:

Step 1: Extend the `uvm_component` Class to Create Your Component

We leverage the UVM developers' work by extending their class `uvm_component`:

```
1    class scoreboard extends uvm_component;
2        `uvm_component_utils(scoreboard);
3
4        virtual interface tinyalu_bfm bfm;
```

Figure 72: Defining the `scoreboard` as a UVM Component

Step 2: Use the `uvm_component_utils() Macro to Register the Class with the Factory.

The `uvm_component_utils() macro registers this class with the factory. Now we'll be able to use the factory to instantiate scoreboard. This is exactly the same macro we used in random_test.

Step 3: Provide the Minimum uvm_component Constructor

All uvm_component classes need a new() method two arguments: name and parent. Here is the scoreboard class's constructor:

```
function new (string name, uvm_component parent);
    super.new(name, parent);
endfunction : new
```

Figure 73: The uvm_component Constructor

The random_test constructor (Figure 68) provided the two required arguments, and also copied the BFM handle into a local variable. UVM component constructors can do more than call super.new(), but they must at least call super.new().

Step 4: Override the UVM Phases as Necessary

When we wrote our UVM test, I created a method called run_phase(), explaining that the UVM would automatically call run_phase() to start the simulation. The run_phase() method was just one of many UVM phase methods.

Every UVM component has these phase methods as part of its inheritance. The UVM builds testbenches and runs them by calling these phase methods in all components in a set order. You define your component by overriding the phase methods and relying upon the UVM to call them in the right order.

You don't need to override the phase methods, but when you do, you should call the super.<phase_method> function as your first step. This ensures that you'll leverage any work done by the UVM developers.

All the phase methods take one argument. This argument must be of type uvm_phase and it must be called phase. There are many UVM phases, but we are going to use only five of them in this primer.

The UVM calls the phase methods in the following order:

- function void build_phase(uvm_phase phase)—The UVM builds your testbench hierarchy from the top down using this method. You must instantiate your uvm_components in this method. If you try to instantiate uvm_components in another method you will get a fatal UVM error.

- function void connect_phase(uvm_phase phase)—The connect phase connects components together. We will learn about connections in a future chapter.

- `function void end_of_elaboration_phase(uvm_phase phase)`—The UVM calls this method after all the components are in place and connected. Use this phase if you need to adjust the testbench after the UVM hierarchy has been set up.

- `task run_phase(uvm_phase phase)`—The UVM calls this task in its own thread. All the `run_phase()` methods in a testbench start running "simultaneously," which means that you don't know which will be launched first.

- `function void report_phase(uvm_phase phase)`—This phase runs after the last objection has been dropped and the test is finished. You use it to report results.

Overriding Methods in the Scoreboard Class

The `scoreboard` class overrides two phase methods: `build_phase()` and `run_phase()`.

Here is the `scoreboard build_phase()` method:

```
36  function void build_phase(uvm_phase phase);
37    if(!uvm_config_db #(virtual tinyalu_bfm)::get(null, "*","bfm", bfm))
38        $fatal("Failed to get BFM");
39  endfunction : build_phase
40
```

Figure 74: The Scoreboard's `build_phase()` Method

All UVM phases have the same `phase` argument. If you do not provide the argument, you will get a compiler error.

In our previous iteration of the testbench, the `uvm_test` object passed the BFM to the verification objects when it created them. This is poor design because it forces someone using the scoreboard to get the BFM for the sole purpose of passing it to other objects. It's better to make each class self-sufficient.

We do that in the `scoreboard` class by getting the BFM from the `uvm_config_db` ourselves in our `build_phase()` method.

Next, we override the `scoreboard`'s `run_phase()` method:

```
15
16    task run_phase(uvm_phase phase);
17      shortint predicted_result;
18      forever begin : self_checker
19        @(posedge bfm.done)
20          case (bfm.op_set)
21            add_op: predicted_result = bfm.A + bfm.B;
22            and_op: predicted_result = bfm.A & bfm.B;
23            xor_op: predicted_result = bfm.A ^ bfm.B;
```

Figure 75: The Scoreboard's `run_phase()` Method

Unlike the other UVM phase methods, all of which are functions, the `run_phase()` method is a task. This means `run_phase()` is the only method that can consume simulation time by waiting for clocks, inserting delays, etc. All other methods must return immediately.

The UVM launches our `run_phase()` method in a thread at the start of the simulation. In the scoreboard's case, the method waits for the edge of the `done` signal and checks the results as in previous versions of this testbench.

This completes the scoreboard's transformation from a generic object to a `uvm_component`. The other three pieces of the testbench have been similarly transformed and are discussed in detail on www.uvmprimer.com. Now we need to build a testbench with them.

Building a Testbench with the `build_phase()` Method

We have just seen how we define a `uvm_component`. This brings us back to our `random_test`. If `random_test` extends `uvm_test` and `uvm_test` extends `uvm_component`, then shouldn't we use the `build_phase()` method to instantiate the three testbench components?

Yes, we should:

```
16   class random_test extends uvm_test;
17      `uvm_component_utils(random_test);
18
19      random_tester   tester_h;
20      coverage        coverage_h;
21      scoreboard      scoreboard_h;
22
23      function void build_phase(uvm_phase phase);
24         tester_h      = new("tester_h", this);
25         coverage_h    = new("coverage_h",    this);
26         scoreboard_h  = new("scoreboard_h",    this);
27      endfunction : build_phase
28
29      function new (string name, uvm_component parent);
30         super.new(name,parent);
31      endfunction : new
32
33   endclass
34
```

Figure 76: Instantiating Testbench Components

Isn't this a nifty little class? All it does is override the build phase and instantiate each of the three testbench components. It doesn't have to worry about doing any of the work because the work gets done in our components' `run_phase()` methods.

In fact, the `random_test` doesn't even have a `run_phase()` method. Its work is done once it's built the test.

The `add_test` class extends the `random_test` class and overrides the `tester_h` data member with a different type. It inherits the `build_phase()` method and so we write `build_phase()` only in one place:

```
1   class add_test extends random_test;
2      `uvm_component_utils(add_test);
3
4      add_tester tester_h;
5
6      function new (string name, uvm_component parent);
7         super.new(name,parent);
8      endfunction : new
9
10  endclass
```

Figure 77: Creating an Add Test Using Extension

UVM Component Summary

In this chapter we learned about the UVM's workhorse class: the `uvm_component`. We stepped through the `uvm_component` creation checklist and defined several component classes.

Whenever we defined a `uvm_component` class we used the `` `uvm_component_utils() `` macro to "register the class with the factory."

Then we created our components without using the factory. What's that about?

In our next chapter we'll introduce another layer of hierarchy: the `uvm_env`, and we'll see how the `uvm_test` and the `uvm_env` work together with the factory to dynamically modify the testbench structure to deliver different tests.

Chapter 13

UVM Environments

In our previous two chapters we learned how the factory can create a top-level object of type `uvm_test` and how that test can instantiate `uvm_components`. We also learned that the UVM automatically calls the phase methods in our components, and that it will automatically launch every component's `run_phase()` method in its own thread.

We used the `uvm_test` and `uvm_components` to create a simple test in which we instantiated the components directly into the test. This concrete approach to creating a test was easy to understand, but it could be difficult to reuse. In fact, it brings us to a discussion of intractable vs. adaptable coding.

Intractable Programming vs. Adaptable Programming

Here's an easy question with an obvious answer: "Given the choice, would you rather write a testbench that gets easier to modify as it gets larger, or harder to modify as it gets larger?"

The correct answer, obviously, is that we'd like our testbenches to get easier to modify as they get larger. We want to be able to add tests and functionality without breaking the testbench, and we'd like to be able to reuse parts of this testbench in the next testbench.

People often talk about reusable coding in terms of "coding this right" and "not coding myself into a corner." These questions are the right ones to be asking, but they don't really frame the question correctly. The real question is whether you are writing intractable code or adaptable code.

Intractable code is code that can be written with little thought but that sets over time, becoming harder and harder to change. The worst case of intractable coding I've ever seen was committed by an engineering team that created new tests by copying all the files in the testbench into another directory, then modifying a couple of files to change the test.

This is the quintessential example of intractable coding, because this testbench clearly got harder to manage as it grew. If this testbench has a bug (and they all have bugs), the person fixing it will have to change the same file in dozens of directories. This person could try modifying the file in one directory and copying it all over, but that will break the testbench if one of the other copies of the file had been modified for some other reason.

This is an intractable nightmare where the testbench breaks every time you touch it, and it can never be reused because you'd need to copy all the directories.

Adaptable coding is coding where everything you write becomes a resource that you can use easily as you expand the testbench. An adaptive testbench gets more powerful as it gets larger because each piece of it provides tools for future work.

Our TinyALU testbench started out intractably when it was all Verilog in a single file. We've been making it more adaptable as we go by applying three basic rules:

* Create classes that do one thing very well and put them together to create solutions.

* Avoid hardcoding behavior where possible.

* Program to interfaces and do not make assumptions about implementation.

Because we've followed these rules, we now have a testbench that doesn't need to be recompiled to run different tests. We can specify the test name on the command line and the factory creates a `uvm_test` object that matches the test name.

However, our `random_test` and `add_test` objects currently violate rule the first rule of adaptable coding. They do two things instead of one:

* They create the testbench structure by instantiating components.

* They modify testbench behavior by declaring different types of testers.

In this chapter, we are going to separate testbench structure from testbench behavior. We're going to add another class, a `uvm_env`, that focuses on creating the testbench structure. Then we'll see how the tests can communicate to that class through the factory.

Architecting Adaptable Code

The TinyALU testbench currently delivers a randomized test and an addition test by defining the `random_tester` class and `add_tester` classes. Let's use these classes to understand the difference between intractable and adaptable programming and how to program adaptably.

Let's first look at the behavior we want from the classes:

* `random_tester`—Send 1000 random operations into the DUT with 1000 different constrained-random operands.

* `add_tester`—Send 1000 add operations into the DUT with 1000 different constrained-random operands.

Here are three ways to implement these classes, from the most intractable to the most adaptable.

The most intractable solution looks like this:

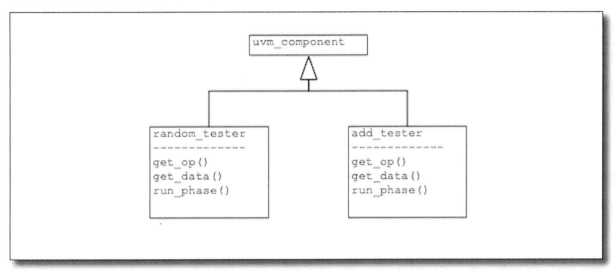

Figure 78: Intractable Solution to Tester Problem

In this solution we've extended the `uvm_component` class twice, once for each tester. Each tester class has a method named `get_op()` that provides the operation, another named `get_data()` that provides the operands, and a third named `run_phase()` that runs 1000 operations through the DUT.

What makes this solution intractable, and thus prone to calcifying and becoming more difficult to modify in the future, is that we've copied the `run_phase()` method in both classes. If we discover an error in the `run_phase`, or want to change its behavior, we need to modify it in multiple places–one file for each class. We could try solving that problem with an include file, but there is a better way.

Here is a more adaptable solution to the problem:

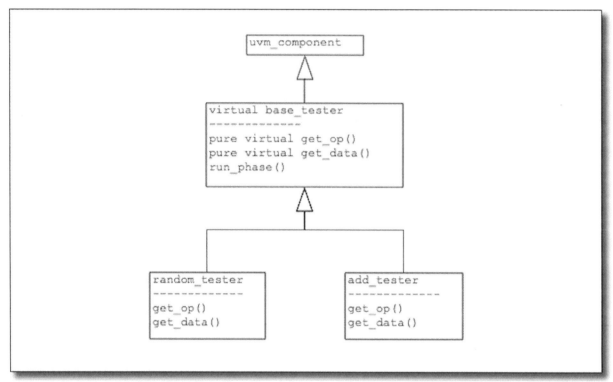

Figure 79: Using a Virtual Class

In this solution we've created a `base_tester` class that provides a `run_phase()` method. The `run_phase()` method delivers 1000 operations using the `get_op()` and `get_data()` methods. The `base_tester` is a virtual class; we cannot instantiate a `base_tester`. Instead we'll extend the `base_tester` to create other tester classes.

The `run_phase()` method assumes that all `base_tester` child classes override the `get_op()` and `get_data()` methods. The `pure virtual` keywords enforce this assumption and the `random_tester` and `add_tester` fulfill it.

This is a better solution, but we can improve upon it. Our goal is to create a testbench that gets easier to modify as it grows because we provide the programmer with more tools. We've created one tool by writing the `base_tester` class—the class sends 1000 transactions to the DUT. Now let's use class extension to create another tool.

The `random_tester` creates random operations and random operands. The `add_tester` creates add operations with random operands. We see that `random_tester` can be a resource for any class that needs random operands or random operations. Let's take advantage of that fact to create a simpler `add_tester`.

Here is the most adaptable solution:

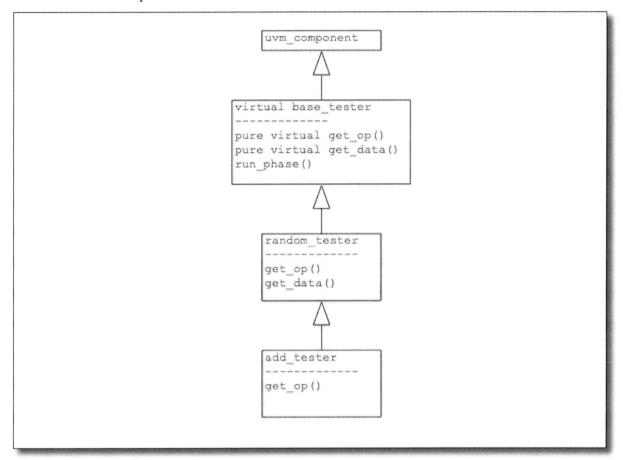

Figure 80: An Adaptable Architecture

We've now turned `random_tester` into a resource for many other tests. One could easily imagine adding classes for `mul_tester` and `xor_tester` to this architecture.

The result is that our `add_tester` code is beautifully simple:

```
1    class add_tester extends random_tester;
2       `uvm_component_utils(add_tester)
3
4       function operation_t get_op();
5          bit [2:0] op_choice;
6          return add_op;
7       endfunction : get_op
8
9       function new (string name, uvm_component parent);
10         super.new(name, parent);
11      endfunction : new
12
13   endclass : add_tester
14
```

Figure 81: The Add Tester Stands on the Shoulders of Giants

We write the `add_tester` by creating a simple `get_op()` method that returns an `add_op` value. We get the rest of our functionality from our lineage. We come from a long line of testers.

Separating Structure from Stimulus

Our `base_tester` class is a nice piece of architecture. It provides a foundation for a family of tester objects that want to send 1000 transactions into the testbench. We've used that foundation to create the `random_tester` class and the `add_tester` class. This raises the question: "How do we use these classes?"

One simple solution is to just keep doing what we did in the previous chapter—we create a family of `uvm_test` classes and declare the `tester` variable to be of a different type in each of them (Figure 77). This solution works but it creates intractable code.

This code is intractable because it hardcodes the structure of the `random_tester` testbench. Every test that extends `random_tester` contains a `random_tester` object, a `coverage` object, and a `scoreboard` object. What would happen if we wanted to create a testbench with a different configuration of testbench objects for different tests? We'd be stuck.

The intractability in this testbench comes from breaking the rule about having each class do one thing. In this case the `random_test` family of classes specifies both the type of the `tester_h` object and the structure of the testbench. We need to split that functionality into two classes.

The UVM solves this problem by providing a class called a UVM Environment (`uvm_env`). The `uvm_env` class extends the `uvm_component` class and provides a standard class to place structural code. The `uvm_env` often contains only the `build_phase()` and `connect_phase()` methods.[16]

We use the `uvm_env` class to hold the structure of the testbench, then we use the test to specify the objects that fulfill that structure. The first step is to instantiate our testbench components in the `env` class then instantiate the `env` class in the random_test class. *[handwritten annotation: env]*

---

[16] More on `connect_phase()` later.

Here is our testbench's UVM hierarchy before and after adding an environment object:

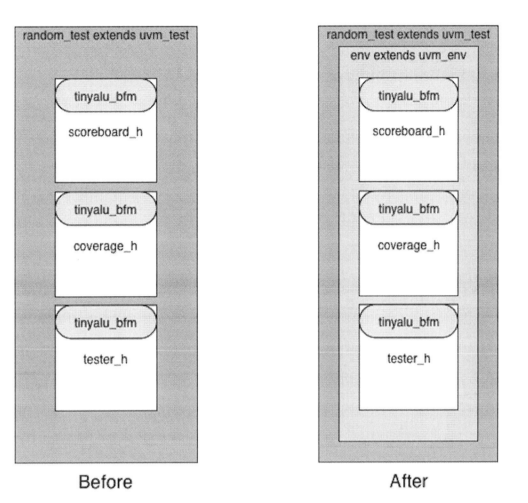

Figure 82: Adding a Structural Level of Hierarchy

The structure above separates our testbench's structure from the `uvm_test`, so we can use the same structure in many tests or in other testbenches.

The `env` Class

The `env` class defines the testbench's structure. It instantiates the object in the testbench, and in a later version will connect them together.

Here is the `env` class definition:

```
1    class env extends uvm_env;
2       `uvm_component_utils(env);
3
4       base_tester    tester_h;
5       coverage       coverage_h;
6       scoreboard     scoreboard_h;
7
8       function void build_phase(uvm_phase phase);
9          tester_h      = base_tester::type_id::create("tester_h",this);
10         coverage_h    = coverage::type_id::create ("coverage_h",this);
11         scoreboard_h = scoreboard::type_id::create("scoreboard_h",this);
12      endfunction : build_phase
13
14      function new (string name, uvm_component parent);
15         super.new(name,parent);
16      endfunction : new
17
18   endclass
```

Figure 83: The Environment Instantiates the Testbench Components

The `env` class demonstrates a wonderful thing about object-oriented programming. The more you break a problem down into single-use classes, the simpler the code gets. A good testbench has many simple classes rather than a few complex classes. This makes debug much easier.

The `env` class simply declares variables to hold three `uvm_components`, `tester_h`, `coverage_h`, and `scoreboard_h`. It instantiates the components in the build phase.

The `build_phase()` method, on the other hand, looks more complicated than the `build_phase()` in the previous chapter (Figure 76). That `build_phase()` called the `new()` method to create its components. This `build_phase()` is calling some complex set of static methods. What's that about?

Creating UVM Components with the UVM Factory

In the Factory Pattern chapter, we learned how to create objects dynamically without hardcoding constructors.

Our simplistic animal factory example (Figure 52) had a severe reuse limitation. Those who wanted to add new animals needed to edit its code. Also, you needed to cast its results to get the object type you wanted.

The UVM factory is much more sophisticated and does away with both of these problems:

- You add new classes to the factory by using the `uvm_component_utils()` and `uvm_object_utils()` macros.

- The factory returns objects of the correct type, so we don't need to cast.

Like all mysterious power from the world beyond, the UVM factory is invoked with a precise incantation. Parts of this incantation vary with the object that we are creating, while others never change:

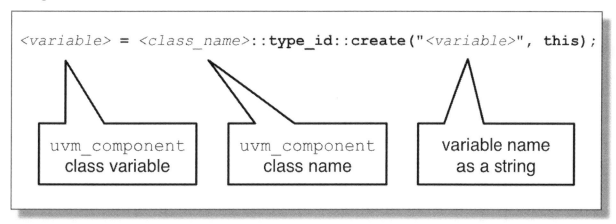

Figure 84: The UVM Factory Incantation

The factory incantation uses the <u>static member/method technique</u> we discussed earlier to deliver a `uvm_component`. Using this incantation has several advantages:

- There is no need to cast the factory output; this is done automatically.

- The compiler catches cases where you didn't define the class or misspelled the class name.

- The compiler catches cases where you forgot to use the `` `uvm_component_utils() `` macro.

Having the compiler catch simple errors saves time, especially when you have a large testbench that takes a long time to initialize.

In our example, we'll use the factory to create the three verification components. Here is the build phase:

```
8       function void build_phase(uvm_phase phase);
9           tester_h     = base_tester::type_id::create("tester_h",this);
10          coverage_h   = coverage::type_id::create ("coverage_h",this);
11          scoreboard_h = scoreboard::type_id::create("scoreboard_h",this);
12      endfunction : build_phase
```

Figure 85: Build Phase Creating Base Tester

The code above uses the factory incantation to create three objects. However, we see one odd thing. The `tester_h` line creates an object of the `base_tester` class. We saw in our class diagrams (Figure 80) that the `base_tester` class is a virtual class. You cannot create a `base_tester`, you must create a child class extended from the base tester. How can this code work?

This code works because the env class is using the `base_tester` variable as a placeholder. The code makes the valid assumption that the factory will return some sort of `base_tester` child class, but it doesn't control the choice of child class. Instead, it relies upon other code to have **overridden** the `base_tester` class in the factory with another class before this `build_phase()` gets called. In our case, this **factory override** gets done in the test class that instantiates this environment.

Overriding the Factory

When we first examined UVM tests, we extended the `random_test` class to create an `add_test`. The `add_test` replaced the `tester` with an `add_tester`.

We created our `add_test` by copying the `random_test` and replacing the `tester` object with an `add_tester` object. This worked, but violated the following rule of thumb:

If you are copying and modifying code, you are doing it wrong.

Copying code always creates intractable code. Someday, someone will modify one of these copies of code and forget to modify the other, and we'll have a bug.

The UVM factory override feature solves this problem.

Since the `add_tester` class extends the `base_tester` class, we can use an `add_tester` wherever we would have used a `base_tester`. This means we can tell the UVM factory to produce an `add_tester` whenever it would have produced a `base_tester` and the code will still compile and run. This is called a **factory override.**

We do this override with another incantation:

```
<base_class_name>::type_id::set_type_override(<child_class_name>::get_type());
```

Figure 86: The Override Incantation

The `set_type_override()` static method tells the factory, "When you see a request for `base_class_name`, return an object of type `new_class_name`."

This feature allows us to separate the structure of the testbench (handled by the `uvm_env` class) from the choice of stimulus (handled by the `uvm_test` class).

For example, here is the `random_test`:

```
1   class random_test extends uvm_test;
2       `uvm_component_utils(random_test);
3
4       env         env_h;
5
6       function void build_phase(uvm_phase phase);
7           base_tester::type_id::set_type_override(random_tester::get_type());
8           env_h = env::type_id::create("env_h",this);
9       endfunction : build_phase
10
11      function new (string name, uvm_component parent);
12          super.new(name,parent);
13      endfunction : new
14
15  endclass
```

Figure 87: Overriding the Tester

This is an adaptable way of writing tests. All tests override the `base_tester` with the tester they need for their stimulus and rely upon the `env` class to create the object and set it in motion. The test class now does one thing very well, and the `env` class does another thing very well.

UVM Environment Summary

In this chapter, we added another level of hierarchy to our UVM testbench by extending the `uvm_env` class. This additional level of hierarchy separated the function of the test (choosing stimulus) from the function of the environment (providing structure.)

We created adaptable code by defining a family of `base_tester` classes and then using the factory and the environment class to choose the tester that would run for each test. We used the factory to allow the test to communicate its stimulus choice to the environment.

In this testbench, all the testbench components access the BFM independently. This is possible in a simple testbench, but it doesn't work in a complex testbench. Complex testbenches are easier to write if our objects can communicate with each other.

The UVM provides a mechanism for this inter-object communication and allows us to connect objects together to create new behavior.

We're going to examine UVM communication in our next four chapters, but first let's digress and talk about how one thinks as an object-oriented programmer.

Chapter 14

A New Paradigm

I first learned about Object-Oriented Programming because I was working at Sun Microsystems when the company introduced Java.[17] I remember reading the first papers on Java, trying some simple programs, and really not getting it.

I remember sitting at my workstation and thinking, "I need a paradigm shift." Sadly, it's almost impossible to create a paradigm shift willfully. You have to keep hacking away until something just clicks and you see the world in a new way.

That said, I hope to give some clues to the Object-Oriented mindset in this chapter and, perhaps, speed up the click.

Objects vs. Scripts

Most of us learned programming in terms of capturing algorithms or procedures in code. We were taught to think of a program as a series of steps, and we'd think of solving a problem in terms of calling a series of commands and subroutines in order to transform data from one representation to another. This is called ***procedural programming***.

Procedural programming is most prevalent in scripting (PERL, Python, etc.) and RTL development. We wait for the positive edge of the clock, and then engage in a series of data transformations that store the results in a series of registers.

The TinyALU VHDL provides an example of procedural thinking in the block that handles single-cycle operations:

```
31    begin
32       if (clk'event and clk = '1') then
33          -- Synchronous Reset
34          if (reset_n = '0') then
35             -- Reset Actions
36             result_aax        <= "0000000000000000";
37          else
38             if START = '1' then
39                case op is
40                   when "001"  =>
41                      result_aax <= ("00000000" & A) +
42                                    ("00000000" & B);
43                   when "010"  =>
44                      result_aax <= unsigned(std_logic_vector("00000000" & A) and
45                                             std_logic_vector("00000000" & B));
```

Figure 88: Procedural Coding

---

[17] In fact, SystemVerilog is a lot like Java.

The code above waits for the positive edge of the clock, decodes the operation, then does the correct operation. A procedural programmer is constantly asking the following question:

What do I do next?

While object-oriented programmers do have to do some procedural thinking, this is not the primary way they approach a problem. They ask a different question:

How do I create and connect objects to solve this problem?

This is a new way to think about programming, but it isn't completely foreign to RTL developers. We connect objects together to solve problems all the time, we just usually call them components in VHDL and modules in Verilog. For example, here is some code from the top level of the TinyALU:

```
119    add_and_xor : single_cycle
120      port map (
121        A            => A,
122        B            => B,
123        clk          => clk,
124        op           => op,
125        reset_n      => reset_n,
126        start        => start_single,
127        done_aax     => done_aax,
128        result_aax   => result_aax
129        );
130    mult          : three_cycle
131      port map (
132        A            => A,
133        B            => B,
134        clk          => clk,
135        reset_n      => reset_n,
136        start        => start_mult,
137        done_mult    => done_mult,
138        result_mult  => result_mult
139        );
140
```

Figure 89: Instantiation in VHDL

In this case we have two components, one that handles single-cycle operations and another that handles three-cycle operations. We've created a TinyALU using the object-oriented programming mindset by answering the question, *"**How do I connect blocks to solve this problem?**"*

In this example we connected the blocks together with signals at the top level of the TinyALU. This brings us to the part of object-oriented programming that I haven't talked about until this point.

How do I connect objects together in the UVM?

Our TinyALU testbench currently has three objects: the `tester_h`, `coverage_h`, and `scoreboard_h`. But, these objects don't talk to each other. In fact they ignore each other, preferring simply to talk to the DUT through their own copy of the BFM.

This will have to change if we want to design complex testbenches using the UVM. We need our objects to communicate.

Two Kinds of Object Communication

Over the course of the next four chapters, we are going to examine two kinds of object communication:

- Single-Thread Communication—In this scenario, an object running in a thread simply calls a method in another object.

- Dual-Thread Communication—In this scenario, two objects are running in different threads. We need both to communicate with the other thread and to coordinate timing between the two threads.

In this spirit of object-oriented design, the UVM provides us with classes that solve these communication problems.

Let's start by looking at single-thread communication, object-oriented design and the `uvm_analysis_port` class.

Chapter 15

Talking to Multiple Objects

Imagine that we are taking a UVM/OOP class and we get this assignment: Write a program that rolls two six-sided dice (2d6) 20 times and prints the following:

- The average dice roll

- A histogram of the dice roll frequency

- A coverage report showing whether we hit all of the possible values from 2-12

It is our goal to write this program using good object-oriented programming techniques. We want our objects to do one thing and to be easily reusable in other contexts. We'll build this program using the UVM.

Let's recall the object-oriented programming mindset question:

How do I create and connect objects to solve this problem?

We need to write classes that solve this problem. Let's start by creating three uvm_components to deliver the three reports. We'll look only at the average class here; the rest are covered in detail on www.uvmprimer.com.

The average class is a uvm_component that gathers data using a method called write() and then prints it out at the end of the simulation using the report_phase():

```
1   class average extends uvm_component;
2       `uvm_component_utils(average);
3
4       protected real dice_total;
5       protected real count;
6
7       function new(string name, uvm_component parent = null);
8           super.new(name,parent);
9           dice_total = 0.0;
10          count = 0.0;
11      endfunction : new
```

Figure 90: The average Class Data Members and Constructor

Average has a data member for the count and another for the dice_total. We protected the data members because no users should be accessing these numbers directly. Now we have to aggregate the total and calculate the average:

```
12
13      function void write(int t);
14          dice_total = dice_total + t;
15          count++;
16      endfunction : write
17
18      function void report_phase(uvm_phase phase);
19          $display ("DICE AVERAGE: %2.1f",dice_total/count);
20      endfunction : report_phase
21   endclass : average
22
```

Figure 91: Calculating and Reporting the Average

We created a write() method[18] that takes in a dice roll number and adds it to dice_total as we increment count.

The UVM calls the report_phase() method when the simulation has completed and we print out the average at that time.

We've also written a histogram class and a coverage class that work similarly to average. They each have a write() method that captures the data and a report_phase() method that outputs the data.

Following good UVM practice, we create a dice_test class that extends uvm_test, and rely upon the UVM to instantiate the test and run it.

Remember, we're looking to connect objects together to solve our problem. So we declare variables at the top of the dice_test class and instantiate the objects:

```
1    class dice_test extends uvm_test;
2       `uvm_component_utils(dice_test);
3
4       dice_roller dice_roller_h;
5       coverage coverage_h;
6       histogram histogram_h;
7       average average_h;
8
9       function void build_phase(uvm_phase phase);
10          coverage_h = new("coverage_h", this);
11          histogram_h = new("histogram_h",this);
12          average_h    = new("average_h",this);
13          dice_roller_h = new("dice_roller_h",this);
14       endfunction : build_phase
```

Figure 92: Declaring and Instantiating Components in the dice_test Class

---

[18] The reason for the name write() will soon become clear.

So far so good. We've defined four classes that solve our dice problem and instantiated them in the build_phase(). This is all according to good UVM and OOP design. Now we just have to run the test. Here is our run_phase():

```
16      task run_phase(uvm_phase phase);
17          int the_roll;
18          phase.raise_objection(this);
19          repeat (20) begin
20              the_roll = dice_roller_h.two_dice();
21              coverage_h.write(the_roll);
22              histogram_h.write(the_roll);
23              average_h.write(the_roll);
24          end
25          phase.drop_objection(this);
26      endtask : run_phase
```

Figure 93: Running the Dice Test

This is a pretty simple-looking program. We repeat a loop 20 times, call the two_dice() method in the dice_roller and pass the roll to each of our reporting objects. The result looks like this:

```
59  # DICE AVERAGE: 6.5
60  #
61  # COVERAGE: 82%
62  #
63  #  2: ##
64  #  3:
65  #  4: ###
66  #  5: ##
67  #  6: ##
68  #  7: ####
69  #  8: ###
70  #  9: ##
71  # 10: #
72  # 11:
73  # 12: #
74  #
```

Figure 94: The Dice Roller Results

Our assignment is complete. We proudly hand in our source code and our results. When the grade comes back, we are shocked to discover that we got a B. B? Why not an A?

We don't normally scrounge for grades, but this is a matter of principle. We storm into the professor's office, brandishing our code.

"We thought we should have gotten an A on this," we say.

"Apparently, I have a different opinion," says our snotty professor.

"Why shouldn't we have an A?"

The professor takes the code from our hand, whips out a red pen and does the following:

```
16
17      task run_phase(uvm_phase phase);
18          int the_roll;
19          super.run_phase(phase);
20          phase.raise_objection(this);
21          repeat (20) begin
22              the_roll = dice_roller_h.two_dice();
23              coverage_h.write(the_roll);
24              histogram_h.write(the_roll);
25              average_h.write(the_roll);
26          end
27          phase.drop_objection(this);
28      endtask : run_phase
29
```

Figure 95: Bad Code, Try Again

The professor says, "This is just scripting. It's not even good scripting. If you were going to script this, you shouldn't have wasted time creating those classes."

Now, we're angry.

"We only made those classes because you told us to."

"Clearly."

"Well, what should we have done?"

"You should have made a set of classes that did one job each and only used the top level here to put them together. Remember the phrase: "How do I **connect** objects together to solve this problem?"

We stare.

The professor continues, "Go investigate the Observer design pattern and the UVM Analysis Port, redo your code, and I'll give you an A."

So it's off to learn about the Observer design pattern.

The Observer Design Pattern

The Observer design pattern could be renamed the Twitter design pattern.

On Twitter, you write a tweet and send it into the world where it goes to people who follow you. You don't need to know who your followers are, and you don't know what your followers will do with the tweet. You don't even have to have any followers to write a tweet. You just write it and press enter.

The same is true with the Observer design pattern. In the Observer design pattern, an object creates data and shares it with the world, not caring how many followers (or observers) it has. Any number of observers can follow the sending object. They all get an identical copy of the data, and they do what they want with it.

How does this apply to our dice problem? We have an object called `dice_roller_h`, and it is creating data that other objects need. The `dice_roller_h` is the observed object and our `coverage_h`, `histogram_h`, and `average_h` objects are our observers. Unfortunately, the UVM calls these objects "subscribers" instead of "observers." (So many synonyms…)

The Observer Design Pattern and the UVM

The UVM provides two classes that make it easy to implement the Observer design pattern:

- `uvm_analysis_port`—Provides a way for any object to send data to a set of subscribers (observers)

- `uvm_subscriber`—An extension to `uvm_component` that allows the component to subscribe to a `uvm_analysis_port`

We'll look at each of these classes in detail here, then use them to rewrite our dice roller.

uvm_analysis_port

The `uvm_analysis_port` allows us to send data to any number of subscribers. We use the port by following a three-step process:

- Declare a variable to hold the analysis port and define the type of data that will travel through it.

- Instantiate the analysis port in the build phase.

- Write data into the analysis port using the `write()` method.

- Once you write the data into the port, it goes to all the subscribers.

The `uvm_analysis_port` has one other method: `connect()`. You call the `connect()` method to connect subscribers to the port. The `connect()` method has one argument: an `analysis_export` object.

uvm_subscriber

The `uvm_subscriber` class extends `uvm_component` and allows you to connect to an analysis port. The class *gives* you something and *requires* something in return:

- The class *gives* you an object called `analysis_export`; you get this by extending the class.

- The class *requires* that you create a method called `write()` that handles the data you receive.

Let's rewrite our dice-rolling objects using these classes.

Implementing Our Subscribers

We have three `uvm_subscribers` in this design: `average`, `coverage`, and `histogram`. Here is the `average` class written as a `uvm_subscriber`:

```
1   class average extends uvm_subscriber #(int);
2       `uvm_component_utils(average);
3
4       real dice_total;
5       real count;
```

Figure 96: Extending the `uvm_subscriber` Class

The only difference between our new code and the previous code is that now we are extending `uvm_subscriber` instead of `uvm_component`. The `uvm_subscriber` class is parameterized—it requires that we provide the type of data that we'll handle. In this case it is an `int`.

Our `write()` method is the same as before.[19] The `write()` method must have a single argument called `t` that is the same type as the type we used in the `uvm_subscriber` extension:

```
12
13      function void write(int t);
14          dice_total = dice_total + t;
15          count++;
16      endfunction : write
17
```

Figure 97: The Subscription Write Method

We make the same change to the `histogram` class and the `coverage` class. We convert them all to `uvm_subscribers`.

Now we need to modify our dice roller and connect the objects together.

Using the `uvm_analysis_port` in the Dice Roller

Earlier we discussed the Observer pattern, which acted like Twitter. We have one object write data, and other objects get copies of the data. We've also seen that the `uvm_analysis_port` allows us to implement the Observer pattern in our classes.

---

[19] Which is why I named it `write()` earlier.

We use the `uvm_analysis_port` by instantiating it in `dice_roller` class like this:

```
1   class dice_roller extends uvm_component;
2      `uvm_component_utils(dice_roller);
3
4      uvm_analysis_port #(int) roll_ap;
5
6      function void build_phase (uvm_phase phase);
7
8         roll_ap = new("roll_ap",this);
9
10      endfunction : build_phase
```

Figure 98: Instantiating the UVM Analysis Port

We declare a variable that holds our analysis port, `roll_ap`. The declaration shows that this analysis port transmits `int` variables. Once we have declared the variable, we instantiate `roll_ap` in our build phase. (You do not use the factory to instantiate ports.)

We now generate dice rolls and write them to an indefinite number of objects, like this:

```
18
19      task run_phase(uvm_phase phase);
20         int the_roll;
21         phase.raise_objection(this);
22         void'(randomize());
23         repeat (20) begin
24            void'(randomize());
25            the_roll = die1 + die2;
26            roll_ap.write(the_roll);
27         end
28         phase.drop_objection(this);
29      endtask : run_phase
30
```

Figure 99: Using the Analysis Port to Send Data

We call the `write()` method in the analysis port and pass it the data. The analysis port then calls the `write()` method in all our subscribers and passes the data. This is the beauty of the analysis port—we don't have to worry about who's using our data, or whether anybody is using it. That's handled in another part of our design.

The `connect_phase()` Method

We've said that the Observer pattern could be called the Twitter pattern. Objects "follow" (subscribe to) other objects to get updates from them. We've created a data source with an analysis port along with several UVM subscribers. Now we need to get the subscribers to follow the data source.

This process is called **connecting objects** and the UVM provides a phase method to do the job. The UVM calls the `connect_phase()` method in all UVM components after it has finished calling all the copies of `build_phase()`.

The UVM calls the `build_phase()` method from the top down. It calls `build_phase()` in the top-level test, then calls `build_phase()` in the objects that test created. After that, it calls `build_phase()` in the new objects that were just created. Eventually it reaches a point in the hierarchy where it has run the `build_phase()` method for all the components.

Once the UVM is done with `build_phase()` it starts at the bottom of the hierarchy and starts calling `connect_phase()` methods. It works from bottom to top until all the objects have had their `connect_phase()` called. We use the `connect_phase()` to connect our UVM subscribers to analysis ports.

There are <u>two pieces to the connection process:</u>

- The `uvm_subscribers` contain an object called `analysis_export`. We do not need to instantiate this object; it is done for us when we extend `uvm_subscriber`.

- The `uvm_analysis_port` class provides a method called `connect()`.

- We make a subscriber subscribe to an analysis port by calling the analysis port's `connect()` method and passing it the `analysis_export` object.

Here is our new `dice_test` with a `connect_phase()` that connects the subscribers to the dice roller:

```
1    class dice_test extends uvm_test;
2       `uvm_component_utils(dice_test);
3
4       dice_roller dice_roller_h;
5       coverage coverage_h;
6       histogram histogram_h;
7       average average_h;
8
24
25      function void connect_phase(uvm_phase phase);
26         dice_roller_h.roll_ap.connect(coverage_h.analysis_export);
27         dice_roller_h.roll_ap.connect(histogram_h.analysis_export);
28         dice_roller_h.roll_ap.connect(average_h.analysis_export);
29      endfunction : connect_phase
30   endclass : dice_test
```

Figure 100: Connecting Subscribers to an Analysis Port

We have three subscribers. Each has an object called `analysis_export`. We have one analysis port in the `dice_roller_h` object. It is called `roll_ap`. We call the `connect()` method on the `roll_ap` object and pass it the `analysis_export` object from each subscriber.

Getting an A Grade

We now have a design that solves this problem by connecting objects together. The dice roller rolls the dice and writes the number to its subscribers. The subscribers create different types of dice statistics. We could add new statistics to the program by writing a new subscriber object and connecting it to the dice roller. Nothing else needs to change.

We'll complete our assignment submission by drawing our designs using an object connection diagram. We use diagrams such as this one to show others how we've connected our classes together:

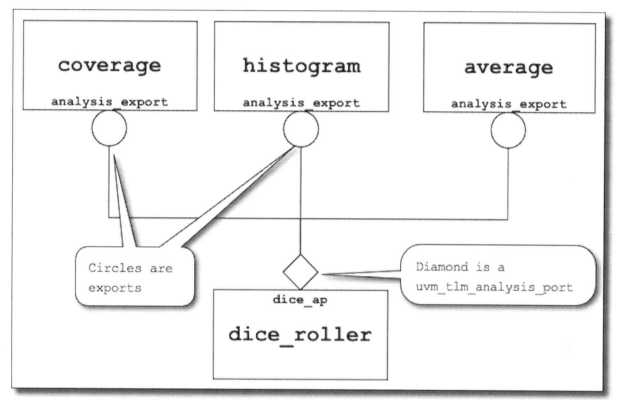

Figure 101: Object Connection Diagram

The diagram shows that our `dice_roller` contains a `uvm_analysis_port` named `dice_ap`, and that each of the subscribers contain an `analysis_export` object. The export objects are always the arguments to the `connect()` method in the port.

Talking to Multiple Components Summary

In this chapter we used the UVM to allow objects to share data. We learned about the Observer pattern and how to implement it by the `uvm_analysis_port` and `uvm_subscriber` classes. We used these classes to get an A in our programming class by writing a dice-rolling analysis program.

In the next chapter, we'll apply analysis ports and subscribers to the UVM testbench.

Chapter 16

Using Analysis Ports in a Testbench

The UVM developers must have implemented the Observer pattern (using `uvm_subscribers` and `uvm_analysis_ports`) for a reason. It's not all dice and histograms. They did it because the Observer pattern is perfect for monitoring a DUT.

All testbenches do two things:

- Drive stimulus through the DUT
- Watch what happens

Our testbench does this with one object that drives stimulus and two objects that watch what happens. The `tester_h` object drives stimulus and the `scoreboard_h` and `coverage_h` objects watch what happens. In UVM parlance, the `scoreboard_h` and `coverage_h` objects make up the testbench's *analysis layer*. Hence the name `uvm_analysis_port`.

In this chapter, we'll see how we use the `uvm_analysis_port` class to create the analysis layer in the TinyALU testbench.

The Duplicate Code Problem

Creating two pieces of code that do essentially the same thing is like opening the tent flap on a camping trip; you're inviting bugs in.

We have a duplicate code problem in our TinyALU testbench in that we have two classes, `coverage_h` and `scoreboard_h`, that need to see TinyALU commands. In our previous versions of the testbench, we gave both of these classes a copy of the BFM and wrote code to extract the command from the signals. But this is bug-inducing duplication.

It's much better to have the BFM detect the commands on the TinyALU pins and pass the data to the scoreboard and coverage objects. The scoreboard also needs the result, so we'll want our BFM to detect results and pass those to the testbench.

We'll solve this problem using analysis ports.

Testbench Diagram

As we move from monolithic code to connected sets of objects, it becomes useful to draw the connections before we start writing the code. Here is a drawing of our new testbench using analysis ports:

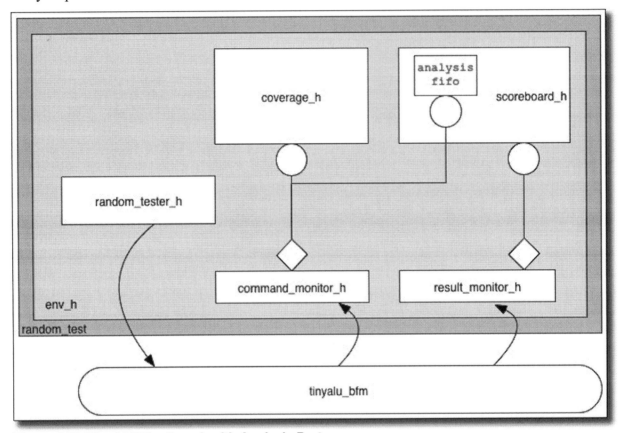

Figure 102: TinyALU Testbench with Analysis Ports

As in previous testbenches, the `tester_h` has a handle to the BFM. However, in this testbench the `tinyalu_bfm` has handles to two new objects, the `command_monitor_h` and the `result_monitor_h`. The BFM recognizes TinyALU commands and results and passes them to these monitors. The monitors, in turn write the data into an analysis port where they go to the `coverage_h` and `scoreboard_h` objects.

The `scoreboard_h` object actually subscribes to two analysis ports: one to get the TinyALU command, and the other to get the TinyALU result.

In this chapter, we'll look at the code that makes all these connections.

Object Handles in the BFM

The great thing about object-oriented programming is that you can add functionality to parts of your testbench by simply sharing the handle to an object. In this case, we're going to connect the `tinyalu_bfm` to the rest of the testbench by using the handle to an object.

First we declare variables in the BFM that can hold the objects:

```
1  interface tinyalu_bfm;
2      import tinyalu_pkg::*;
3
4      command_monitor command_monitor_h;
5      result_monitor  result_monitor_h;
```

Figure 103: Declaring Class Handles in the BFM

We defined the `command_monitor` and `result_monitor` classes in the `tinyalu_pkg` along with the rest of the classes. We've imported that `tinyalu_pkg` into the `tinyalu_bfm` and can now declare variables that hold object handles.

We set the `command_monitor_h` and `result_monitor_h` variables from within the monitors' `build_phase()` methods. Here is the `command_monitor` copying a handle of itself into the `command_monitor_h` variable in the BFM:

```
1   class command_monitor extends uvm_component;
2       `uvm_component_utils(command_monitor);
3
4   uvm_analysis_port #(command_s) ap;
5
6   function void build_phase(uvm_phase phase);
7       virtual interface tinyalu_bfm bfm;
8
9       if(!uvm_config_db #(virtual interface tinyalu_bfm)::get(null, "*","bfm", bfm))
10          $fatal("Failed to get BFM");
11
12      bfm.command_monitor_h = this;
13
14      ap  = new("ap",this);
15
16  endfunction : build_phase
17
```

Figure 104: Copying the `command_monitor` Handle into the BFM

The code above gets the handle to the BFM from the UVM configuration database and then copies its own handle (`this`) into the variable in the BFM. Now the BFM can pass data to the testbench through the `command_monitor_h` handle.

The `result_monitor` class does the same thing with the `result_monitor_h` handle.

Monitoring the TinyALU Commands

We monitor the TinyALU commands and results with two `always` blocks called `cmd_monitor` and `rslt_monitor`. Here is the `cmd_monitor` loop:

```
76    always @(posedge clk) begin : cmd_monitor
77       bit new_command;
78       if (!start)
79          new_command = 1;
80       else
81          if (new_command) begin
82             command_monitor_h.write_to_monitor(A, B, op);
83             new_command = (op == 3'b000); // handle no_op
84          end
85    end : cmd_monitor
```

In Interface

Figure 105: Command Monitor in BFM

The `cmd_monitor` loop implements a simple state machine. At the positive edge of the clock, the loop checks the `start` signal. If the `start` signal is high, then we check to see if this is a new command. If it is, then we send it to the testbench by calling the `command_monitor`'s `write_to_monitor()` method.

The result monitor loop is similar:

```
96    always @(posedge clk) begin : rslt_monitor
97          if (done)
98             result_monitor_h.write_to_monitor(result);
99    end : rslt_monitor
```

Figure 106: Result Monitor in BFM

Handling Commands with `command_monitor_h`

The `command_monitor` class takes command data from the BFM, encapsulates it in a struct and passes it through the analysis port. Here is the struct we use to store command data. It is called `command_s`:

```
15    typedef struct {
16       byte unsigned      A;
17       byte unsigned      B;
18       operation_t op;
19    } command_s;
20
```

Figure 107: The `command_s` Struct

The `write_to_monitor()` method populates this struct, then sends it to the testbench through an analysis port:

```systemverilog
1   class command_monitor extends uvm_component;
2     `uvm_component_utils(command_monitor);
3
4     uvm_analysis_port #(command_s) ap;
5
6     function void build_phase(uvm_phase phase);
7       tinyalu_pkg::bfm_g.command_monitor_h = this;
8       ap = new("ap",this);
9     endfunction : build_phase
10
11    function void write_to_monitor(byte A, byte B, bit[2:0] op);
12      command_s cmd;
13      cmd.A = A;
14      cmd.B = B;
15      cmd.op = op2enum(op);
16      $display("COMMAND MONITOR: A:0x%2h B:0x%2h op: %s", A, B, cmd.op.name());
17      ap.write(cmd);
18    endfunction : write_to_monitor
```

Figure 108: Sending Commands with the Analysis Port

This class declares an analysis port that accepts `command_s` structs, instantiates it in the `build_phase()` method, and uses it to send commands into the testbench in the `write_to_monitor()` method.

Our code is getting simpler and clearer as we continue to break operations down into smaller units. This simple conduit code allows us to create a much simpler coverage class. Let's look at that class next.

The TinyALU Coverage Class as a Subscriber

Thanks to the `command_monitor` class, we now have a single source for any object that wants to see the TinyALU commands. All the class has to do is subscribe to the `command_monitor`'s analysis port and implement the `write()` method. This allows us to create simple, easy to debug, and easy to reuse classes. In this case, we're creating a coverage class:

```
1   class coverage extends uvm_subscriber #(command_s);
2       `uvm_component_utils(coverage)
3
4       byte        unsigned     A;
5       byte        unsigned     B;
6       operation_t op_set;
7
8       covergroup op_cov;
```

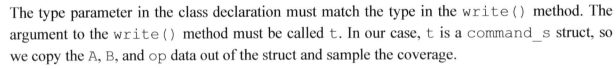
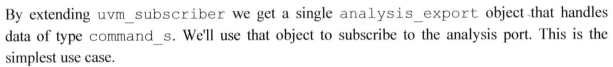

```
58      function void write(command_s t);
59          A = t.A;
60          B = t.B;
61          op_set = t.op;
62          op_cov.sample();
63          zeros_or_ones_on_ops.sample();
64      endfunction : write
65
66  endclass : coverage
67
```

Figure 109: The New, Simpler Coverage Class

The coverage class no longer has to sully itself touching signals, clocks, and bits. Instead it receives a nice clean `command_s` struct from the `command_monitor`'s analysis port.

The type parameter in the class declaration must match the type in the `write()` method. The argument to the `write()` method must be called `t`. In our case, `t` is a `command_s` struct, so we copy the `A`, `B`, and `op` data out of the struct and sample the coverage.

By extending `uvm_subscriber` we get a single `analysis_export` object that handles data of type `command_s`. We'll use that object to subscribe to the analysis port. This is the simplest use case.

The scoreboard class is more complicated in that it needs to subscribe to two different analysis ports (see Figure 102.)

Subscribing to Multiple Analysis Ports

The basic UVM analysis port mechanism allows one `uvm_subscriber` to subscribe to one analysis port. However, there are cases, such as in the `scoreboard`, where we want one `uvm_subscriber` to get data from two analysis ports.

The simplest way to solve this problem is to instantiate another subscriber object within our class and let that object subscribe to the second port. The UVM provides a class called `uvm_tlm_analysis_fifo` that solves this problem.

If we want to subscribe to two different analysis ports, we'll need two different `analysis_export` objects to pass to each analysis port's `connect()` method. In the case of the `scoreboard`, we need an `analysis_export` for `command_s` data and an `analysis_export` for `shortint` data. Here is how we create `analysis_exports` for both:

```
1  class scoreboard extends uvm_subscriber #(shortint);
2     `uvm_component_utils(scoreboard);
3
4     uvm_tlm_analysis_fifo #(command_s) cmd_f;
5
6     function void build_phase(uvm_phase phase);
7        cmd_f = new ("cmd_f", this);
8     endfunction : build_phase
```

Figure 110: Creating Subscribers for Two Classes

The scoreboard class extends `uvm_subscriber` using the `shortint` type. This means that the `scoreboard's write()` method must accept `shortint` data and we have an `analysis_export` for `shortint` data.

However, our scoreboard needs to accept both `shortint` data and `command_s` data. We've dealt with the `shortint`, so now we need to deal with the `command_s`. We'll do that using the `uvm_tlm_analysis_fifo`.

The `uvm_tlm_analysis_fifo` is a parameterized class that provides an `analysis_export` on one side, and a `try_get()` method on the other side. We use the `analysis_export` to subscribe to the `analysis_port` we need and we use the `try_get()` method to pull data out of the FIFO.

In this example we declared a `uvm_tlm_analysis_fifo` that accepts `command_s` structs and we pull data out of it in our `run_phase()` method. This gives us a way to subscribe to two kinds of data in the same class.

The `scoreboard`'s `write()` method assumes that we will only get a result after a command has gone into the system. When the `result_monitor` passes us a result, we pull commands off the FIFO until we find one that isn't a `no_op` or `rst_op`. We use that command to make a prediction and compare it to the result. Here is the code:

```
10   function void write(shortint t);
         shortint predicted_result;
         command_s cmd;
         cmd.op = no_op;
14       do
15         if (!cmd_f.try_get(cmd)) $fatal(1, "No command in self checker");
16       while ((cmd.op == no_op) || (cmd.op == rst_op));
17
18       case (cmd.op)
19         add_op: predicted_result = cmd.A + cmd.B;
20         and_op: predicted_result = cmd.A & cmd.B;
21         xor_op: predicted_result = cmd.A ^ cmd.B;
22         mul_op: predicted_result = cmd.A * cmd.B;
23       endcase // case (op_set)
24
25       if (predicted_result != t)
26         $error (
27       "FAILED: A: %2h  B: %2h  op: %s actual result: %4h    expected: %4h",
28           cmd.A, cmd.B, cmd.op.name(), t,  predicted_result);
29   endfunction : write
30
```

Figure 111: The Scoreboard Does Its Thing in a `write()` Method

The FIFO's `try_get()` method reads a command out of the FIFO. The method returns 0 if the FIFO is empty; since it should never be empty, we throw a fatal exception if that ever happens.

We use the `do...while()` loop to read through the commands until we get one that actually does something. This must be the command that created our result. We use it to make a prediction and compare.

Now we have two monitor classes and two analysis classes. All that's left is to connect the monitors to the analysis tools.

Subscribing to Monitors

We connect the analysis objects to the monitors using the `connect_phase()` method in `env`:

```
24       function void connect_phase(uvm_phase phase);
25         result_monitor_h.ap.connect(scoreboard_h.analysis_export);
26         command_monitor_h.ap.connect(scoreboard_h.cmd_f.analysis_export);
27         command_monitor_h.ap.connect(coverage_h.analysis_export);
28       endfunction : connect_phase
```

Figure 112: Subscribing to Monitors

The `coverage_h` object and `scoreboard_h` object each have an `analysis_export`. We call the `connect()` method in the correct analysis ports to connect these subscribers to their port. The scoreboard also contains the `cmd_f` analysis FIFO. We use the FIFO's `analysis_export` object to connect the scoreboard to the `command_monitor` (highlighted).

Summary of Subscribers and Analysis

In this chapter, we used the `uvm_analysis_port` to implement the Observer pattern in our testbench. We saw how we could consolidate all the signal-level monitoring in the BFM and use monitor classes and analysis ports to pass the monitor data to any number of analysis classes.

Communicating between objects using the `uvm_analysis_port` is an example of intrathread communication. All the function calls happen within a single thread. When the `cmd_monitor` `always` block calls `write_to_monitor()` it is actually calling all the `write()` methods in all the subscribers within its thread.

Intrathread communication such as this is useful for cases such as analysis. But we often need to pass information between threads. We'll see that this can be tricky, but the UVM gives us the tools to do it easily.

Chapter 17

Interthread Communication

The phrase "interthread communication" seems like a scary Java term, but it is something that we Verilog and VHDL engineers have been doing from day one. Everything we do when we write HDL is based on multiple threads (`initial`, `always`, and `process` blocks) and their communication.

Consider a producer/consumer program written in SystemVerilog. The producer module creates numbers, and the consumer module reads numbers:

```
1   module producer(output byte shared, input bit put_it, output bit get_it);
2       initial
3           repeat(3) begin
4               $display("Sent %0d", ++shared);
5               get_it = ~get_it;
6               @(put_it);
7           end
8   endmodule : producer
9
10  module consumer(input byte shared,  output bit put_it, input bit get_it);
11      initial
12          forever begin
13              @(get_it);
14              $display("Received: %0d", shared);
15              put_it = ~put_it;
16          end
17  endmodule : consumer
18
19  module top;
20      byte shared;
21      producer p (shared, put_it, get_it);
22      consumer c (shared, put_it, get_it);
23  endmodule : top
```

Figure 113: Module-Based Interthread Communication

The `initial` blocks in the `producer` and `consumer` are two threads. Interthread communication simply describes the fact that we can send data from one thread to the other using the ports on the modules. We send the data across the `shared` bus and use the `put_it` and `get_it` signals to suspend each thread so the other thread can run.

The `producer` module thread writes data into the `shared` variable and toggles the `get_it` signal to tell the `consumer` module that the data is ready. Then the `producer` blocks on the `put_it` signal so the `consumer` can get the data. The `consumer` initially blocks on the `get_it` signal, waiting for a command from the `producer`. When the `producer` toggles the `get_it` signal, the `consumer` wakes up and reads the data from the `shared` variable and toggles the `put_it` signal to release the `producer`. Then the `consumer` blocks on the `get_it` signal again to wait for the next datum.

The result is communication:

```
22    # Loading work.top(fast)
23    # Sent 1
24    # Received: 1
25    # Sent 2
26    # Received: 2
27    # Sent 3
28    # Received: 3
```

Figure 114: Successful Module Communication

In this chapter, we'll learn how to do the same thing with objects in the UVM.

Wait. There Are No Object Ports?

The threads in our previous example communicated through the ports in our `producer` and `consumer` modules. We used the ports to pass both the `shared` variable between the module and the communication signals.

Object-oriented SystemVerilog does not have a built-in language construct such as module ports. Instead, SystemVerilog provides the ability to share handles between objects, and it delivers thread-coordinating constructs such as semaphores and mailboxes.

One could create a thread communication system using these building blocks, but then everyone's solution would be slightly different. The UVM has solved this problem by providing a universal solution to interthread communication that hides the details. The solution has two basic parts:

- Ports—Objects we instantiate in our `uvm_components` to allow our `run_phase()` task to communicate with other threads. We use put ports to send data to other threads and get ports to receive data from other threads.

- TLM FIFOs—Objects that connect a put port with a get port. TLM stands for Transaction-Level Modeling. This name is an artifact of previous versions of the UVM. While TLM FIFOs may move transactions (as we'll see later), they can move any data type.

TLM FIFOs hold only one element. While this is a pretty lame capacity for a FIFO, it is quite useful for interthread communication.

In this chapter, we'll recreate our module-based producer/consumer using ports and FIFOS.

The Producer as an Object

In our module-based example (Figure 113), the producer created three numbers and sent them to the consumer using the module's ports to send the data and coordination signals (put_it and get_it). In order to do the same thing in an object, we need to declare and instantiate an object of type uvm_put_port:

```
1   class producer extends uvm_component;
2       `uvm_component_utils(producer);
3
4       int shared;
5       uvm_put_port #(int) put_port_h;
6
7       function void build_phase(uvm_phase phase);
8           put_port_h = new("put_port_h", this);
9       endfunction : build_phase
```

Figure 115: Declaring and Instantiating a Put Port

The uvm_put_port is a parameterized class; we need to tell it the type of data that will be traveling through it. In this case, we are sending data of type int.

The object put_port_h can now take int data and pass it to a FIFO. Here is our producer sending three numbers using the put port:

```
16
17      task run_phase(uvm_phase phase);
18          phase.raise_objection(this);
19          repeat (3) begin
20              put_port_h.put(++shared);
21              $display("Sent %0d", shared);
22          end
23          phase.drop_objection(this);
24      endtask : run_phase
25  endclass : producer
26
```

Figure 116: Sending Data from the Producer Object

This is exactly like the module-based code (Figure 113), except that it's simpler. The module-based code had to mess with the get_it and put_it signals to handle the interthread communication. In this case, the put_port_h object handles all that. The first time through the loop we call the put() method to put the data into the port. This moves the data into the FIFO. Now the FIFO is full. We loop around and call put() to store the next number, but since the FIFO is full, put() blocks us. We'll remain blocked until the consumer gets the data out of the FIFO.

The Consumer as an Object

The consumer declares and instantiates a `uvm_get_port` object to get data out of the FIFO:

```
1  class consumer extends uvm_component;
2     `uvm_component_utils(consumer);
3
4     uvm_get_port #(int) get_port_h;
5     int shared;
6
7     function void build_phase(uvm_phase phase);
8        get_port_h = new("get_port_h", this);
9     endfunction : build_phase
```

Figure 117: Declaring and Instantiating a Get Port

The `uvm_get_port` is also a parameterized class. It is up to us to declare the `get_port_h` variable using the same type that we used in our producer's put port.

Once we have the port, we use it in our `run_phase()` thread to get data from the producer:

```
16        task run_phase(uvm_phase phase);
17           forever begin
18              get_port_h.get(shared);
19              $display("Received: %0d", shared);
20           end
21        endtask : run_phase
22  endclass : consumer
```

Figure 118: Receiving Data from the Producer

As in the producer, the `uvm_get_port` handles all the interthread coordination. When this task starts, we call `get()` to get the data out of the port, but since the FIFO is empty, the `get()` method blocks us. The `producer` fills the FIFO and blocks. At that point we wake up and get the data out of the FIFO. We loop around and try to get more data out of the FIFO, but the FIFO is empty again, so we block again.

In short, the system works like this:

- The producer fills the FIFO and suspends, allowing

- the consumer to empty the FIFO and suspend, allowing the

- producer to fill the FIFO and suspend, allowing the

- etc.

Now all we have to do is connect the ports using this all-powerful FIFO.

Connecting Ports

In our module example (Figure 113), we connected the producer to the consumer by instantiating them in a top-level module and connecting their ports. We'll do something similar here by instantiating the `producer`, `consumer`, and `tlm_fifo` in a `uvm_test` and connecting their port objects to the `tlm_fifo`.

Here is the instantiation:

```
1    class communication_test extends uvm_test;
2        `uvm_component_utils(communication_test)
3
4        producer producer_h;
5        consumer consumer_h;
6        uvm_tlm_fifo #(int) fifo_h;
7
8        function void build_phase(uvm_phase phase);
9            producer_h = new("producer_h", this);
10           consumer_h = new("consumer_h", this);
11           fifo_h = new("fifo_h",this);
12       endfunction : build_phase
```

Figure 119: Instantiating the Producer, Consumer, and TLM FIFO

Notice that the `uvm_tlm_fifo` has the same type parameter as the producer's put port and the consumer's get port.

The UVM calls `build_phase()` in all objects from the top down. So it first instantiates the `producer_h`, `consumer_h`, and `fifo_h` objects, then it calls their build methods. The `producer_h` and `consumer_h build_phase()` methods instantiate the ports in these objects.

Once all the build phase methods have been called, the UVM calls the components' `connect_phase()` methods starting at the bottom of the hierarchy.

Connecting the Ports to the TLM FIFO

In previous chapters we learned that the `uvm_analysis_port` object had `connect()` method and that the `connect()` method took an object called `analysis_export` as an argument. We also learned that the `uvm_subscriber` class provided the `analysis_export` object.

The same approach works for put ports, get ports, and the `uvm_tlm_fifo`. The `uvm_tlm_fifo` provides two objects: `put_export` and `get_export`. You connect the `uvm_tlm_fifo` to ports by passing these objects to the ports' connect methods:

```
18       function void connect_phase(uvm_phase phase);
19           producer_h.put_port_h.connect(fifo_h.put_export);
20           consumer_h.get_port_h.connect(fifo_h.get_export);
21
22       endfunction : connect_phase
23   endclass : communication_test
```

Figure 120: Connecting Ports to the FIFO

Our `connect_phase()` method reaches down into the producer and consumer to reference the ports and call their `connect()` methods. The `fifo_h` object contains a `put_export` object and a `get_export` object. We pass these objects to the ports to create the connection.

The result is communication:

```
58    # Sent 1
59    # Received: 1
60    # Sent 2
61    # Received: 2
62    # Sent 3
63    # Received: 3
```

Figure 121: Communication Using Objects Instead of Modules

Communication without Blocking

The blocking communication style we used above works great as long as you don't have to worry about clocks or time. If you have one time-free thread talking to another time-free thread, you can block on your `get()` and `put()` calls and never run into trouble.

However, blocking on your `get()` and `put()` calls does not work when you are also blocking on some other event such as a clock edge. You'd run into trouble doing that because a clock-driven system assumes that you will always be ready to run at the edge of a clock and that you won't block on anything else.

The UVM handles this problem by providing non-blocking versions of `put()` and `get()`. They are called `try_put()` and `try_get()`.

The `try_put()` and `try_get()` methods work just like `put()` and `get()` except they never block. Instead, they return a bit that tells you whether the put or get were successful. It's your job to test the bit and do the right thing. (You may recall that we saw `try_get()` in action in the previous chapter. We used it in the scoreboard's `write()` method in Figure 111.)

Let's modify our producer and consumer a bit to demonstrate using `try_get()`. In this example, we'll give the consumer a 14 ns clock edge to work with and we'll have the producer deliver data with a delay of 17 ns per write.

Here is the consumer using `try_get()` with a clock:

```
14    task run_phase(uvm_phase phase);
15        super.run_phase(phase);
16        forever begin
17            @(posedge clk_bfm_i.clk);
18            if(get_port_h.try_get(shared))
19                $display("%0tns  Received: %0d", $time,shared);
20        end
21    endtask : run_phase
22
```

Figure 122: A Consumer with a Clock

This consumer has a forever loop, but blocks on the positive edge of a clock. At each positive edge of the clock, it tries to get data from the FIFO. If `try_get()` returns a 1 (meaning it got data), the consumer prints out the data. If `try_get()` returns a 0, the consumer loops back around and waits for the next positive clock edge.

Here is our timed communication:

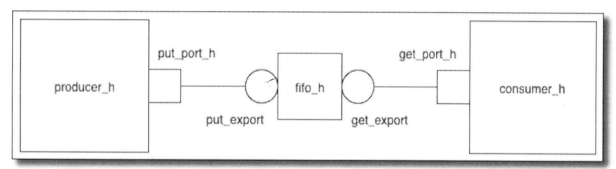

```
59    # 17ns   Sent 1
60    # 21ns   Received: 1
61    # 34ns   Sent 2
62    # 35ns   Received: 2
63    # 51ns   Sent 3
64    # 63ns   Received: 3
```

Figure 123: Non-Blocking Interthread Communication

We see that the consumer is running on a clock that creates a positive edge at 7 ns and then creates another every 14 ns after that. The producer is producing data every 17 ns. The consumer only takes the data on its clock edges. It only prints to the screen when it gets data.

Drawing the Put Ports and Get Ports

In our previous chapter we drew a picture of the testbench using a diamond to represent the analysis port and a circle to represent the analysis export. We can draw a similar diagram with put ports and get ports, except that we use a square for the put ports and get ports. The exports remain circles:

Figure 124: Producer/Consumer Drawing

We draw put/get port relationships with squares, while we draw analysis port relationships with diamonds. We'll see why in the next chapter. We don't distinguish between blocking and non-blocking put and get functions.

Interthread Communication Summary

In this chapter we learned that interthread communication between objects is similar to interthread communication between modules. We learned that the UVM provides an interthread communication mechanism in terms of `uvm_put_ports`, `uvm_get_ports`, and `uvm_tlm_fifos`. We saw that any object that wants to communicate to another thread must instantiate a port and that the ports must be connected to FIFOs.

In our next chapter, we're going to use this interthread communication to break our testbench down into smaller pieces. We're going to separate test stimulus generation from driving the DUT.

Chapter 18

Put and Get Ports in Action

In the previous chapter, we learned how to create interthread communication using put and get ports. In this chapter we'll add that functionality to our TinyALU testbench.

Throughout this book we've looked for places where one object is handling multiple functions, and then teased those functions apart into multiple classes. Classes that handle one function are easier to debug and reuse.

In this chapter, we'll look at our `base_tester` class (and by extension the `random_tester` and `add_tester` classes). Our `base_tester` does two things. It chooses the types of operations we apply to the testbench and it applies them using the BFM. We're going to split that operation into two classes, one to choose the operation and the other to interact with the BFM. We'll see later that this division allows much more flexibility in the way our testbench operates.

Our new testbench will look like this:

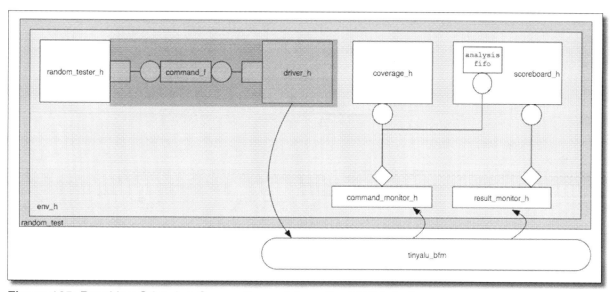

Figure 125: Breaking Stimulus Generation out from the BFM Interface

The shaded portion of the testbench is new. The term ***driver*** refers to an object that takes data from the testbench and converts it to signals on the BFM. We've added a `driver_h` object to our testbench and connected it to the `tester_h` object using a FIFO. Now our testbench has a class devoted to choosing stimulus and another devoted to delivering it.

Here is the `env_h` object connecting these objects:

```
1   class env extends uvm_env;
2       `uvm_component_utils(env);
3
4       random_tester      random_tester_h;
5       driver        driver_h;
6       uvm_tlm_fifo #(command_s) command_f;
...
24
25      function void connect_phase(uvm_phase phase);
26          driver_h.command_port.connect(command_f.get_export);
27          random_tester_h.command_port.connect(command_f.put_export);
28
29          result_monitor_h.ap.connect(scoreboard_h.analysis_export);
30
```

Figure 126: Declaring and Connecting the Tester and Driver

We've now got a `tester`, a `driver`, and a `uvm_tlm_fifo` that accepts `command_s` structs. We've added a put port to the `tester` and called it `command_port` and a get port to the driver and also called it `command_port`. Then we passed the `get_export` and `put_export` objects from the FIFO to their respective `connect()` methods.

It's sometimes difficult to remember the exact incantation for connecting ports to exports. Just remember that "Ports connect to exports." You always pass an export to the port's `connect()` method.

Let's take a look inside the objects.

The `base_tester` Class

The earlier wisdom of creating a `base_tester` class is proving itself out now. The connection between the `base_tester` and the `driver` doesn't affect the `get_op()` or `get_data()` methods, so the `random_tester` and `add_tester` remain unchanged. They will inherit the new functionality.

The `base_tester` is identical to its previous incarnations except that it doesn't contain a handle to the BFM. Instead it contains a `uvm_put_port` called `command_port`. We declare and instantiate the put port:

```
1   virtual class base_tester extends uvm_component;
2   `uvm_component_utils(base_tester)
3     virtual tinyalu_bfm bfm;
4
5     uvm_put_port #(command_s) command_port;
6
7     function void build_phase(uvm_phase phase);
8       command_port = new("command_port", this);
9     endfunction : build_phase
10
11    pure virtual function operation_t get_op();
```

Figure 127: Declaring and Instantiating a Put Port in Tester

Now that we have a put port, we use it to send data to the testbench:

```
36    task run_phase(uvm_phase phase);
37      byte         unsigned        iA;
38      byte         unsigned        iB;
39      operation_t                  op_set;
40      command_s    command;
41
42      phase.raise_objection(this);
43      command.op = rst_op;
44      command_port.put(command);
45      repeat (1000) begin : random_loop
46        command.op = get_op();
47        command.A =  get_data();
48        command.B =  get_data();
49        command_port.put(command);
50      end : random_loop
51      #500;
52      phase.drop_objection(this);
53
54    endtask : run_phase
55
```

Figure 128: Tester Using a Put Port

The `base_tester` declares a `command_s` variable, loads it up with an operation and data and sends it into the testbench through the put port. Once we put the data into the put port, we don't worry about it anymore; that's someone else's job.

On large complex testbenches, this division of labor is a lifesaver because creating the right data is a difficult task, and the person doing it doesn't want to have to worry about signal-level considerations. That's the driver class's job.

The TinyALU Driver

The driver is a simple class that pulls commands out of a get port and sends them to the BFM through the BFM's `send_op` task. Here is the driver:

```
1   class driver extends uvm_component;
2       `uvm_component_utils(driver)
3
4       virtual interface tinyalu_bfm bfm;
5
6       uvm_get_port #(command_s) command_port;
7
8       function void build_phase(uvm_phase phase);
9           if(!uvm_config_db #(virtual interface tinyalu_bfm)::get(null, "*","bfm
10              $fatal("Failed to get BFM");
11          command_port = new("command_port",this);
12      endfunction : build_phase
13
14      task run_phase(uvm_phase phase);
15          command_s       command;
16          shortint        result;
17
18          forever begin : command_loop
19              command_port.get(command);
20              bfm.send_op(command.A, command.B, command.op, result);
21          end : command_loop
22      endtask : run_phase
23
```

Figure 129: The TinyALU Driver with Get Port

The driver loops forever, taking commands off the get port and sending them to the BFM. If there is no command in the `get_port`, the driver blocks and the tester supplies a new command.

Summary of Using Ports in the TinyALU Testbench

In this chapter we adopted the UVM interthread communication classes to further refine our TinyALU testbench. We now have a testbench with separate stimulus and analysis functions, and we've further broken the stimulus function down into stimulus generation (the tester classes) and stimulus application (the driver class).

We've now got the technology to easily drive tons of stimulus through a testbench and capture it in the analysis layer. This brings up the question of what to do with all that data. To this point we've been using the SystemVerilog `$display`, `$error`, and `$fatal` system calls, but these are crude devices for managing the amount of data generated by a modern testbench.

We need more powerful reporting tools, and the UVM delivers them. In our next chapter we'll examine UVM reporting tools.

Chapter 19

UVM Reporting

Ivan Pavlov is most famous for getting dogs to salivate when he rang a bell, but this was not what won him a Nobel Prize. Pavlov won the Nobel Prize for research into digestion. He'd feed dogs, then take samples from their digestive system as the food passed through their bodies.

We engineers often do the same thing, but with data. We pass data into our DUT through the testbench and watch it come out the other end. When there's a problem, we need to be able to print data samples to the screen.

Testbenches generate a lot of data. If we use unfiltered printing tools such as `$display()`, we are quickly overwhelmed with messages. There's no way to figure out what's going on because there's simply too much output.

The UVM provides a reporting system to address this problem. All `uvm_components` provide methods for reporting. We print to the screen using three UVM reporting macros, and we control the output by calling the methods in the `end_of_elaboration_phase()`.

Let's look at the output macros first.

UVM Reporting Macros

The UVM delivers four reporting macros that display messages of increasing severity:

- `` `uvm_info(<Message ID String>, <Message String>, <Verbosity>) ``
- `` `uvm_warning(<Message ID String>, <Message String>) ``
- `` `uvm_error(<Message ID String>, <Message String>) ``
- `` `uvm_fatal(<Message ID String>,<Message String>) ``

Before looking at the arguments for these macros, let's look at two of them in use. This will give us a feel for how the macros work before we look at the details. The code below is from the `scoreboard` class:

```
33
34        data_str = $sformatf(" %2h %0s %2h = %4h (%4h predicted)",
35                            cmd.A, cmd.op.name() ,cmd.B, t,  predicted_result);
36
37        if (predicted_result != t)
38          `uvm_error ("SCOREBOARD", {"FAIL: ",data_str})
39            else
40          `uvm_info ( "SCOREBOARD", {"PASS: ",data_str}, UVM_HIGH)
41
```

Figure 130: Using UVM Reporting in the Scoreboard

The code above demonstrates how we use the UVM reporting macros and fill in the arguments. There are four pieces to look at:

- Severity—Clearly an error is more serious than an informational message. The UVM recognizes this by providing four levels of severity in the names of the four macros: info, warning, error, fatal.

- Message ID String—The "SCOREBOARD" string identifies the type of message. The UVM reports the number of times each ID generated a message. We can also use the ID to control the UVM's actions associated with a message.

- Message String—The Message String contains our message to the reader. In this case, we've concatenated the "PASS" or "FAIL" string to the data_str string. We created the data_str string using $sformatf().

- Verbosity—Only the `uvm_info() macro has a verbosity argument. This argument controls whether this message gets printed. We'll examine verbosity later.

When we run a test with 10 random operations, we get the following output:

```
132   # UVM_ERROR tb_classes/scoreboard.svh(38) @ 510:
...   uvm_test_top.env_h.scoreboard_h [SCOREBOARD] FAIL:  4f add_op ff = 014e (014f
...   predicted)
```

Figure 131: Uh Oh, This is Not Good

The predicted response didn't match the actual, so we called the `uvm_error() macro and created the above output. This example shows the typical fields of a UVM message:

- UVM_ERROR—the message's severity
- tb_classes/tinyalu...—the call's file and line number
- @ 510—the time of the error measured in simulation time
- uvm_test_top.env_h.scoreboard_h—the call's location in the UVM hierarchy
- [SCOREBOARD]—the message ID we supplied
- FAIL: 4f add_op...—the message string we created using $sformatf()

All UVM reporting macros create messages that follow this format; the only difference among them is the severity.

When we ran the test, I said that we had executed 10 commands, and when we look at Figure 130 we see a `uvm_info() macro that should be called if a test passed. However, our test output only showed the error. Why is that?

This is because the `uvm_info() message has a verbosity of UVM_HIGH. This is keeping it from printing. Verbosity control is one of the keys to the UVM Reporting system. Let's examine it now.

UVM Verbosity Levels

The `uvm_info()` macro has three arguments. The third is called *verbosity*. Verbosity handles a problem we've all seen when we debug: too many messages.

It's common for us to place debugging statements in our code. These are usually `$display()` statements (in SystemVerilog), and they print out data that helps us debug. However, when we're done debugging we either have to comment out these statements or suffer with pages of spurious information. UVM verbosity solves this problem.

The UVM uses two steps to control messages:

- We provide the verbosity in all our `uvm_info()` macro calls.

- We set the verbosity ceiling[20] for our simulation. We control our output by setting the ceiling for our simulation, either globally or for a specific part of the UVM hierarchy.

The UVM ships with six built-in verbosity levels:

```
305    typedef enum
306    {
307        UVM_NONE   = 0,
308        UVM_LOW    = 100,
309        UVM_MEDIUM = 200,
310        UVM_HIGH   = 300,
311        UVM_FULL   = 400,
312        UVM_DEBUG  = 500
313    } uvm_verbosity;
```

Figure 132: The UVM Verbosity Levels

The UVM's default ceiling is UVM_MEDIUM. If you don't change the verbosity ceiling, any information message with a verbosity above UVM_MEDIUM will not print. We can now see why our passing messages aren't printing.

```
39         else
40           `uvm_info ( "SCOREBOARD", {"PASS: ",data_str}, UVM_HIGH)
```

Figure 133: A True Debug Message

The information message has a verbosity set to UVM_HIGH, which corresponds to 300. The default verbosity in the testbench is UVM_MEDIUM; this is 200. Since 300 is greater than 200, the message doesn't fit under the ceiling and doesn't print.

If we want to see messages when our commands work properly, we'll need to raise the verbosity ceiling to UVM_HIGH.

---

[20] The UVM developers called this ceiling the verbosity level, but the word ceiling is more descriptive.

Setting the Verbosity Ceiling (Level)

We control the number of `` `uvm_info() `` messages we see by setting the verbosity ceiling. If we lower the ceiling, fewer messages will get under it. If we raise the ceiling, more messages get under it.

We can control the ceiling two ways: globally for the whole simulation, and locally for a specific branch of the UVM hierarchy.

Setting the Global Verbosity Ceiling

We control the verbosity globally with the +UVM_VERBOSITY plusarg. If we want to see our passing messages in the `scoreboard`, we raise the verbosity like this:

```
8   vsim top_optim -coverage +UVM_TESTNAME=random_test +UVM_VERBOSITY=UVM_HIGH
```

Figure 134: Setting Global Verbosity

The +UVM_VERBOSITY plusarg sets the default verbosity ceiling for the entire simulation. The string UVM_HIGH comes from the values in the uvm_verbosity enumerated type. We see there our message's verbosity of UVM_HIGH.

Setting the Verbosity Ceiling in the UVM Hierarchy

Setting the verbosity ceiling globally is easy, but it could lead to information overload in a large testbench. If you're working with 20 other engineers on a project, they will all have their own debug statements with a high verbosity, and raising the ceiling will open the floodgates (to mix metaphors.)

Fortunately, the UVM developers have thought of this. All uvm_components provide report control methods, including ones that control the verbosity ceiling. These come in two flavors. One flavor controls reporting for one component; the other controls reporting for that component and all beneath it in the hierarchy.

When I speak about hierarchy, I am not speaking about the module hierarchy in the DUT. Instead I'm talking about the hierarchy the UVM created when it called the `build_phase()` method in all instantiated components. For example, here is the UVM hierarchy for this chapter's example:

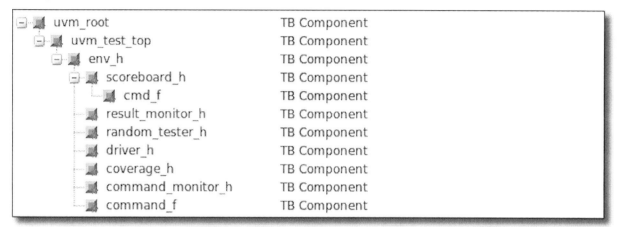

Figure 135: UVM Hierarchy for TinyALU Testbench[21]

If we want to use the UVM hierarchy to control the verbosity ceiling, we need to call our reporting methods after the hierarchy has been built, but before the simulation starts running. We do this using a UVM phase method that runs just before the `run_phase()` method—the `end_of_elaboration_phase()` method.

In the example below, we use the `end_of_elaboration_phase()` method in the `env` to set the verbosity ceiling for the `scoreboard` component and everything below it in the hierarchy:

```
23
24      function void end_of_elaboration_phase(uvm_phase phase);
25          scoreboard_h.set_report_verbosity_level_hier(UVM_HIGH);
26      endfunction : end_of_elaboration_phase
27
```

Figure 136: Setting the Verbosity Ceiling in the Scoreboard

The `set_report_verbosity_level_hier()` method[22] above sets the verbosity ceiling for the `scoreboard_h` component and everything below it in the hierarchy. If we wanted to set the verbosity only for `scoreboard_h`, we would have made the same call without the "_hier" suffix (`set_report_verbosity_level(UVM_HIGH)`).

---

[21] This is a screen shot from Mentor Graphics' Questa Verification Platform. Mentor Graphics owns the copyright to this and all screenshots of Questa's GUI or output formats and has given me permission to reprint them in this book.

[22] Again the UVM developers use the word *level* rather than *ceiling*.

Here is the output when we run with higher verbosity:

```
106  # UVM_INFO @ 0: reporter [RNTST] Running test random_test...
107  # UVM_INFO tb_classes/scoreboard.svh(37) @ 130:
...  uvm_test_top.env_h.scoreboard_h [SCOREBOARD] PASS:  09 mul_op ff = 08f7 (08f7
...  predicted)
108  # UVM_ERROR tb_classes/scoreboard.svh(35) @ 210:
...  uvm_test_top.env_h.scoreboard_h [SCOREBOARD] FAIL:  c5 add_op e5 = 01aa (01ab
...  predicted)
109  # UVM_INFO verilog_src/uvm-1.1c/src/base/uvm_objection.svh(1121) @ 791:
...  reporter [TEST_DONE] 'run' phase is ready to proceed to the 'extract' phase
```

Figure 137: Scoreboard Output Showing Passes

Now our `scoreboard_h` component outputs results on both passes and fails. We can see that the multiplication command passes just fine, and a little work with our hex calculator tells us that it does indeed have the right answer.

The `scoreboard` component doesn't do as well with the `add_op`. We can see that the predicted value doesn't match the actual result, but our calculator tells us that the actual result is correct. Our scoreboard has a bug.

In our small testbench we would simply go into the scoreboard and fix it. But in a large testbench with a complicated scoreboard, we wouldn't have the knowledge to fix the scoreboards. We would file a bug against it, disable it until it is fixed, and move on.

How do we disable the `scoreboard_h` error messages? The first thought might be that we lower the verbosity ceiling to zero, and that will block all messages. This won't work because the verbosity ceiling only works on `uvm_info()` messages. Stopping `uvm_error()` messages requires stronger medicine.

Disabling Warning, Error, and Fatal Messages

Warning messages, error messages, and fatal messages are immune from the verbosity ceiling's puny attempts to silence them. In order to stop these messages, we need to use another control knob of UVM reporting called **actions**.

The UVM reporting macros can do more than write to the screen. In fact, writing to the screen is only one of six things they can do:

```
277  typedef enum
278  {
279    UVM_NO_ACTION = 'b000000,
280    UVM_DISPLAY   = 'b000001,
281    UVM_LOG       = 'b000010,
282    UVM_COUNT     = 'b000100,
283    UVM_EXIT      = 'b001000,
284    UVM_CALL_HOOK = 'b010000,
285    UVM_STOP      = 'b100000
286  } uvm_action_type;
287
```

Figure 138: The UVM Reporting Actions

We can control which levels of severity invoke which actions, and we can create multiple actions by ORing the above actions together. The details of the actions are beyond the scope of this primer. In our case, we are simply going to use the `UVM_NO_ACTION` to disable errors in our scoreboard:

```
23
24      function void end_of_elaboration_phase(uvm_phase phase);
25          scoreboard_h.set_report_severity_action_hier(UVM_ERROR, UVM_NO_ACTION);
26      endfunction : end_of_elaboration_phase
27
```

Figure 139: Disabling Errors in the Scoreboard

The above code controls the `scoreboard` component and everything below it. The call to `set_report_severity_action_hier()` tells the reporting system to do nothing on message with a severity of ERROR (`` `uvm_error() ``).

The result is blessed silence:

```
106     # UVM_INFO @ 0: reporter [RNTST] Running test random_test...
107     # UVM_INFO verilog_src/uvm-1.1c/src/base/uvm_objection.svh(1121) @ 791:
        reporter [TEST_DONE] 'run' phase is ready to proceed to the 'extract' phase
108     #
109     # --- UVM Report Summary ---
110     #
111     # ** Report counts by severity
112     # UVM_INFO :    4
113     # UVM_WARNING :    0
```

Figure 140: If Only This Worked on People

The simulation ran with no messages and no complaints. Once the `scoreboard` is fixed, we can turn the error messages back on.

UVM Reporting Summary

In this chapter we created messages using the UVM's reporting system. The reporting system is essential to managing messages from large testbenches and allows us to create debug messages and leave them in our code.

We've been journeying through the UVM by converting the TinyALU testbench from a monolithic HDL-style testbench to a modular object-oriented testbench. We've learned how to manipulate and display data using a variety of objects. However, the data itself has been exempted from being converted into classes.

This will now change. There are tremendous advantages to representing our data as classes and objects, and so we will now turn to transaction-level modeling. But first we're going to examine another object-oriented programming concept: Deep Operations.

Chapter 20

Class Hierarchies and Deep Operations

Life has very few hard and fast rules, but it has some. These include "never eat anything bigger than your head," "never eat the yellow snow," and "never create multiple copies of the same code."

Worded differently, "If you find yourself copying code and making small modifications to it, you are doing something wrong."

We can think of object-oriented programming as a gigantic effort to keep people from copying code. Instead of copying and reusing code, we either extend classes (as we do when we extend `uvm_component`) or we create an instance of an object (as we do when we create a `uvm_put_port`).

Even with these tools, we must be ever vigilant against code that breaks our ability to leverage other people's code. This is especially true of ***deep operations***. As an example, let's look at copying.

Again with the Lions

The lions are back, and this time they are going to help us understand deep operations. Consider the following class hierarchy:

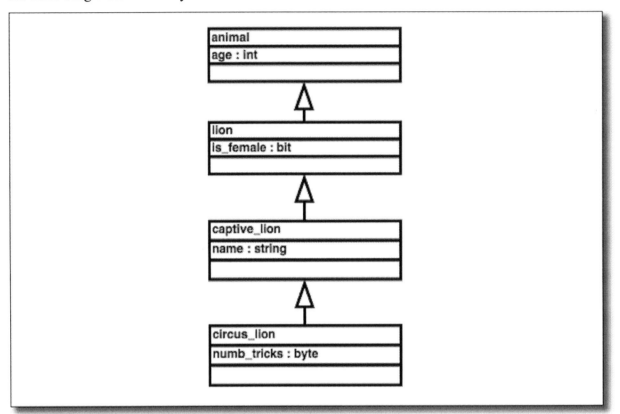

Figure 141: The Lion's Class Hierarchy

This hierarchy goes from the most general (animal) through to the most specific (circus_lion). Each class adds a bit of information that makes sense only for that level of detail. The challenge appears when we want to use all that information.

Consider a method called convert2string(). We'll be using this handy method many times in the rest of the book. The method takes the values in an object and converts them to a string suitable for printing.

This simple function shows how easily we can fall into the copied-code trap. Here is the convert2string() method for the animal class:

```
 8      virtual function string convert2string();
 9         return $sformatf("Age: %0d", age);
10      endfunction : convert2string
11
```

Figure 142: Weird Science: Converting an animal to a String

The animal class has only one variable, `age`, so we convert that variable to a string and return it. So far so good. But what happens when we want to convert a `lion` to a `string`? Here is one approach:

```
27      function string convert2string();
28          string gender_s;
29          gender_s = (is_female) ? "Female" : "Male";
30          return sformat("Age: %0d Gender: ",age, gender_s);
31      endfunction : convert2string
32
```

Figure 143: Handling Gender Proactively in Our Lion

This `convert2string()` method interprets the `is_female` bit for us by turning it into the word "Female" or "Male." Then it also prints the age. That seems nice. What happens when we get to `captive_lion`?

```
51
52      function string convert2string();
53          return {$sformatf("age: %0d is_female: %0b name: %s",
54                  age, is_female, name) };
55      endfunction : convert2string
56
```

Figure 144: The Perils of Copied Code

Well, this is awkward. The person who defined the `captive_lion` class chose not to give us the nifty conversion to "Female" and "Male." We just get the bit. Now we have an extension of a class that acts differently from its parents.

The problem is that we're copying code from class to class. With each copy we get the chance to introduce errors or different interpretations of the code. But an even worse problem looms.

Consider what happens if we change our class hierarchy to this:

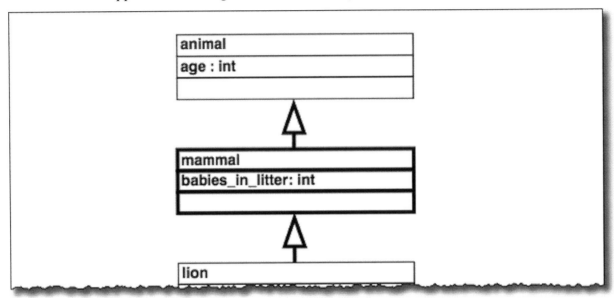

Figure 145: Surprise! Someone Changed the Lion Hierarchy

Someone has introduced another level of hierarchy with a new variable. The `captive_lion` `convert2string()` method is now broken. It doesn't display all the variables. We now have a bug in code we didn't touch.

It seems unjust, but we deserved to get that bug as punishment for copying code. For shame!

What should we have done instead? We should have used a deep approach to writing our `convert2string()` method and let each class worry about its own variables. We can do this by using the `super` keyword to refer to variables and methods in our parent class, rather than in our class. Let's redo the `convert2string()` method using a deep approach.

The animal `convert2string()` stays the same, but we do something different in the `mammal convert2string()`:

```
25
26      function string convert2string();
27         return {super.convert2string(),
28                 $sformatf("\nbabies in litter: %0d",babies_in_litter)};
29      endfunction : convert2string
30
31
```

Figure 146: Using a Deep Strategy for String Conversion

Now we don't have to worry about what's in the `animal` class because `super.convert2string()` handles that. We worry only about mammal's `babies_in_litter` variable. The chain continues with the lion class:

```
49    function string convert2string();
50        string gender_s;
51        gender_s = (is_female) ? "Female" : "Male";
52        return {super.convert2string(), "\nGender: ",gender_s};
53    endfunction : convert2string
54
55
```

Figure 147: Using `super` to Print `mammal` and `animal` Information

Our call to `super` calls the `convert2string()` method in `mammal`, which in turn calls the `convert2string()` method in `animal`. This code climbs the class hierarchy to build the strings. As an added benefit, anyone who extends the lion class automatically accesses the bit to string conversion we do in this method.

Here is the result:

```
112    initial begin
113        circus_lion1_h = new(.age(2), .is_female(1),
114                             .babies_in_litter(2), .name("Agnes"),
115                             .numb_tricks(2));
116        $display("\n--- Lion 1 ---\n",circus_lion1_h.convert2string());
117        circus_lion2_h = new();
```

```
24    # --- Lion 1 ---
25    # Age: 2
26    # babies in litter: 2
27    # Gender: Female
28    # Name: Agnes
29    # numb_tricks: 2
30    #
```

Figure 148: Printing a Circus Lion

We know that any class in the lion hierarchy will print properly because of our deep `convert2string()` method.

Deep Copying

Copying objects is not as easy as you might think. A simple assignment such as `obj2_h = obj1_h` does not create a new copy of the object in `obj2_h`. Instead, both variables contain the handle to the same object. **If you change the object using one handle, you're also changing the object pointed to by the other handle because both handles point at the same object.**

In order to create a true copy of an object, you need to instantiate a new object and copy the data from one object into the other like this:

```
112    initial begin
113        circus_lion1_h = new(.age(2), .is_female(1),
114                              .babies_in_litter(2), .name("Agnus"),
115                              .numb_tricks(2));
116        $display("\n--- Lion 1 ---\n",circus_lion1_h.convert2string());
117        circus_lion2_h = new();
118        $display("\n--- Lion 2 before copy ---\n",
119                  circus_lion2_h.convert2string());
120        circus_lion2_h.do_copy(circus_lion1_h);
121        $display("\n--- Lion 2 after copy ---\n",
122                  circus_lion2_h.convert2string());
123    end
```

Figure 149: Copying a Lion

In the above code we create `circus_lion1_h` and load it with data. Then we create `circus_lion2_h`. Finally we copy the data from `circus_lion1_h` into `circus_lion2_h` using the `do_copy()` method.

The `do_copy()` method suffers from the same challenge as the `convert2string()` method. Each class can copy only the variables defined in that class. It must rely upon calling `super.do_copy()` to copy parent variables.

Here is the challenge in creating a deep `do_copy()` method. Each class in the hierarchy must call the class above it, so all the `do_copy()` methods need to take the same type of argument as input. But almost by definition, the `do_copy()` method for a `circus_lion` is going to want to take a `circus_lion` variable as an input and the `do_copy()` in the `captive_lion` class is going to want to take a `captive_lion` as an argument.

We have a conundrum.

We can solve this problem with polymorphism. We'll take advantage of the fact that all the do_copy() methods in this family of classes take some descendent of the animal class. So we'll use animal class as the argument to do_copy(). This gives us the following do_copy() methods in `circus_lion` and `captive_lion`:

```
64   class captive_lion extends lion;
65       string name;

76       function void do_copy(animal copied_animal);
77           captive_lion copied_captive_lion;
78           super.do_copy(copied_animal);
79           $cast(copied_captive_lion, copied_animal);
80           this.name = copied_captive_lion.name;
81       endfunction : do_copy
82   endclass : captive_lion
83
84   class circus_lion extends captive_lion;
85       byte numb_tricks;

98       function void do_copy(animal copied_animal);
99           circus_lion copied_circus_lion;
100          super.do_copy(copied_animal);
101          $cast(copied_circus_lion, copied_animal);
102          this.numb_tricks = copied_circus_lion.numb_tricks;
103      endfunction : do_copy
104  endclass : circus_lion
```

Figure 150: Using Polymorphism to Implement Deep Copies

The do_copy() methods in `captive_lion` and `circus_lion` both take an animal (copied_animal) as an argument. They also declare a variable of their own type (copied_captive_lion and copied_circus_lion.)

Both methods work the same way. They immediately pass the copied_animal variable to their parent class's do_copy() method. This works because all the do_copy() methods take animal as their argument.

After calling their parents, they cast copied_animal into a variable of their type. So circus_lion's do_copy() casts copied_animal into copied_circus_lion, and captive_lion's do_copy() casts copied_animal into copied_captive_lion.

This works because a `circus_lion` is a `captive_lion`, so a `circus_lion` can be stored in a `captive_lion` variable.

After the `do_copy()` casts the animal into the appropriate lion, it copies the data from the copied lion into `this` object. We can keep adding levels into this class hierarchy as long as each class follows this pattern for its `do_copy()`.

The result is a happily copied lion:

```
23  #
24  # --- Lion 1 ---
25  # Age: 2
26  # babies in litter: 2
27  # Gender: Female
28  # Name: Agnus
29  # numb_tricks: 2
30  #
31  # --- Lion 2 before copy ---
32  # Age: 0
33  # babies in litter: 0
34  # Gender: Male
35  # Name:
36  # numb_tricks: 0
37  #
38  # --- Lion 2 after copy ---
39  # Age: 2
40  # babies in litter: 2
41  # Gender: Female
42  # Name: Agnus
43  # numb_tricks: 2
44
```

Figure 151: Copied Lions

We print out Lion 2 before and after we copy, because we are verification engineers and we want to make sure the copy actually happened.

Summary of Deep Operations

In this chapter we learned how to implement deep operations in a class hierarchy. We saw that copying code between classes can easily lead to bugs and we saw that a variety of methods can use `super` to implement deep operations.

We also found another use for polymorphism as we created a `do_copy()` method that had the same argument type on the entire class hierarchy.

In our next chapter, we'll see how the UVM uses deep operations when we begin moving data around the testbench in objects called UVM Transactions.

Chapter 21

UVM Transactions

Throughout this primer, we've been breaking the TinyALU testbench into smaller pieces to improve its debugability and adaptability. Each class does one thing and passes its data on to another class to do its work, so it's easy to understand the class and find errors.

We've modularized our work by providing methods in each class that do the work of that class and by being careful to avoid situations where one class needs to know the internal workings of another.

This has all been excellent work, except for one thing. We didn't apply any of the object-oriented programming goodness to our data. We are still passing commands into the testbench using the `command_s` struct, and reading results with the `shortint` type. It's time to fix that. Life could be so much better with objects.

Advantages of Storing Data in Objects

One could (and very well might) argue that there's no need to store our data in objects. The `command_s` struct is nice and modular and the `shortint` is only a number. Why mess with success?

Once again the answer comes down to adaptability, debug, and reuse. Consider the case of printing command data. Any class that wants to use the data from the `command_s` needs to know that that `command_s` consists of three fields: A, B and op, and that A and B are `byte unsigned` types while op is an `operation_t` type.

Even our little testbench uses this information in several places: `tester` uses it, `driver` uses it, `coverage` uses it, and `scoreboard` uses it. This means that our code has a weak spot. A modification to the `command_s` struct requires modifications all over the testbench.

Also, remember that the TinyALU commands are simple relative to other designs. An Ethernet command structure would be much more complex, and if you needed to reuse that testbench for another form of Ethernet, you'd have a huge job ahead of you.

You might argue that storing the command data in a class is exactly like storing it in a struct. Both have data fields and encapsulate the data. However the class, and the objects we instantiate from that class, have two advantages the structs cannot match:

Classes have methods that interact with the data and hide details from users.
We work with objects through handles, and we can pass these handles around our testbench. Therefore several objects can easily share a piece of data. This is important when we have large data items such as video frames.

We implement these advantages using the UVM class library to get the power to develop a much better testbench.

Transaction Power...Activate!

It's time to stop talking about "classes and objects that store data" and start using the industry term *transactions*. When we define a data-storing class, we say that we are "defining a transaction," and when we deliver a data-storing object around, we say we are "delivering a transaction."

Truth be told, "transaction" is one of those squishy, overloaded words that infest the lexicon of digital verification (others are "scoreboard" and "virtual"). I guarantee you that someone will read my definition of "transaction" above and say, "That's not a transaction. A transaction is ..." and they'll deliver some slightly different definition. I say we let them have their fun while we move on.

Transactions encapsulate both data and all the operations we can do to that data. These operations include the following:

- Providing a string with the data values in it (`convert2string`)

- Copying another transaction of the same class into this transaction (`do_copy`)

- Comparing this transaction to another of the same class (`do_compare`)

- Randomizing the data fields (using SystemVerilog's built-in `randomize` method)

- Encapsulating all this data in the transaction makes the rest of the testbench much simpler. For example, `tester` won't need to figure out legal values to drive the testbench. It will simply let the transaction randomize itself

Defining Transactions

We define transactions by extending the `uvm_transaction` base class and writing the following methods:

- `do_copy()`

- `do_compare()`

- `convert2string()`

We're going to walk through all these steps by converting our old `command_s` struct into a new class called `command_transaction`. We'll start with our data fields.

Creating Randomized Data Fields

In our first testbench iteration we created two testing functions called `get_op()` and `get_data()`. We needed these functions to get a reasonable distribution of randomized input data. The `get_op()` function handled the fact that the operation bus has eight possible values, but only six legal operations. The `get_data()` function gave us a 1/3 chance of having all zeros, all ones, or randomized data on the A and B busses. Without it we'd have a 1/256 chance of getting all zeros, and that would make it difficult to reach our coverage goals.

The truth is, these functions were unnecessary because SystemVerilog handles all these randomization issues if we use the `rand` keyword when we declare our variables.

Here is the top of our new `command_transaction` class:

```
 1   class command_transaction extends uvm_transaction;
 2       `uvm_object_utils(command_transaction)
 3       rand byte unsigned      A;
 4       rand byte unsigned      B;
 5       rand operation_t        op;
 6
 7       constraint data { A dist {8'h00:=1, [8'h01 : 8'hFE]:=1, 8'hFF:=1};
 8                         B dist {8'h00:=1, [8'h01 : 8'hFE]:=1, 8'hFF:=1};}
 9
10
```

Figure 152: Declaring and Constraining Random Variables in the Command Transaction

Our new transaction declares the A, B, and `op` data members as random variables using the `rand` keyword. All SystemVerilog classes provide an implicit method called `randomize()` that chooses a random number for the class's random variables.

SystemVerilog allows us to get rid of the `get_op()` and `get_data()` functions. We no longer need the `get_op()` because SystemVerilog will set the `op` variable to one of the six enumerated values, all of which are legal.

We replace the `get_data()` function with a SystemVerilog constraint.[23] The `constraint` statement gives us an equal chance of choosing all zeros, all ones, or a random number in between.

The `uvm_object` Constructor

The `uvm_transaction` class extends `uvm_object`, not `uvm_component`. So it has a simpler constructor. Since UVM objects are not in the UVM hierarchy, the constructor does not need a parent handle, only a name.

Therefore our `uvm_transaction` constructor looks like this:

```
65       function new (string name = "");
66           super.new(name);
67       endfunction : new
68
69   endclass : command_transaction
70
```

Figure 153: The Simple `uvm_object` Constructor

It is good form to give our objects a name, but the testbench will survive if we don't.

---

[23] The details of SystemVerilog constraints are beyond the scope of this book. I discuss constraints in detail in the book *FPGA Simulation*.

The `do_copy()` Method

The `uvm_object` class and all its descendants provide a `copy()` method that copies one object's data into another object of the same type, and a `clone()` method that returns a new instance of an object with all the same data.

These methods work only if we override a method called `do_copy()`. The `do_copy()` method works exactly like the one we wrote for our lions. The only difference is that the UVM requires that we call the argument `rhs`. This stands for Right Hand Side to represent the position of the data in an assignment such as `lhs = rhs`:

```
12    function void do_copy(uvm_object rhs);
13        command_transaction copied_transaction_h;
14
15        if(rhs == null)
16          `uvm_fatal("COMMAND TRANSACTION", "Tried to copy from a null pointer")
17
18        if(!$cast(copied_transaction_h,rhs))
19          `uvm_fatal("COMMAND TRANSACTION", "Tried to copy wrong type.")
20
21        super.do_copy(rhs); // copy all parent class data
22
23        A = copied_transaction_h.A;
24        B = copied_transaction_h.B;
25        op = copied_transaction_h.op;
26
27    endfunction : do_copy
```

Figure 154: Implementing `do_copy()` in Our Transaction

First we check to make sure that we weren't passed a null handle. If we were, then we fatal out.

Next we check to make sure that the `rhs` variable holds an object of our type. We cast `rhs` to `copied_transaction_h`. If the cast returns 0, then we have been passed an object of class other than `command_transaction`. We can't copy something other than our own class, so we fatal out. These kinds of checks make debugging much easier.

Now that we know that we've got an object of the right type, we call `super.do_copy()` to pass the object up to our parent class and let it copy all its data. Once that's done, we copy the data from the `copied_transaction_h` object into our A, B, and op data members.

The `clone_me()` Method and MOOCOW

One of the best things about using transactions is that multiple objects can see the same data if they have handles to the same object. This may not seem so great in the TinyALU, but if you're designing a massive switch with 250 ports, you might not want to have 250 copies of the same data.

However, this notion of sharing a single object using multiple handles works only if your team religiously implements a design rule called Mandatory Obligatory Object Copy On Write

(MOOCOW[24])MOOCOW means that you can share a handle to an object as long as you're not going to change the data in the object (thus changing it for everyone without them knowing about it). As soon as you want to *Write* to the object, you are obliged to manually make a *Copy* of the object, thus Manual Obligatory Object Copy On Write (MOOCOW)..

The UVM supports MOOCOW with a method called `clone()`. The `clone()` method leverages your `do_copy()` method to create a second copy of an object—a clone. The `clone()` method returns a `uvm_object`. You need to cast the returned object into your target class.

This creates a situation where everybody who clones an object needs to provide their own `$cast` call, so I like to create a convenience routine called `clone_me()` that clones the object and does the cast:

```
29      function command_transaction clone_me();
30          command_transaction clone;
31          uvm_object tmp;
32
33          tmp = this.clone();
34          $cast(clone, tmp);
35          return clone;
36      endfunction : clone_me
```

Figure 155: The `clone_me()` Method

The method simply clones the current object, casts the clone to this object type, and returns the object using the correct class. We don't use this method in the TinyALU testbench because we never need to worry about MOOCOW.

The `do_compare()` Method

We compare a lot of data in testbenches, so it's reasonable to assume that a `uvm_transaction` can compare itself to another `uvm_transaction`. The UVM provides the `compare()` method to do this (`compare()` returns 1 if the two objects are the same).

We implement the `uvm_transaction`'s `compare()` method by providing a `do_compare()` method in our class. The `do_compare()` method compares this transaction to another like it. This is a deep comparison, so we pass the method's arguments to our parent class and roll the result into our comparison.

---

[24] Yes. It is a tortured acronym, but it's easy to remember so we'll forgive those who invented it.

Here is the do_compare() method for the command_transaction:

```
39    function bit do_compare(uvm_object rhs, uvm_comparer comparer);
40      command_transaction compared_transaction_h;
41      bit    same;
42
43      if (rhs==null) `uvm_fatal("RANDOM TRANSACTION",
44                                "Tried to do comparison to a null pointer");
45
46      if (!$cast(compared_transaction_h,rhs))
47        same = 0;
48      else
49        same = super.do_compare(rhs, comparer) &&
50                (compared_transaction_h.A == A) &&
51                (compared_transaction_h.B == B) &&
52                (compared_transaction_h.op == op);
53
54      return same;
55    endfunction : do_compare
56
```

Figure 156: Doing a UVM Comparison

The do_compare() method has two arguments. The first, rhs, is the object we will compare to ourselves. The second is something called a uvm_comparer. The uvm_comparer is beyond the scope of this book, so we'll just pass it to our parent class with rhs when we call super.do_compare().

The method sets a bit called same to 1'b1 if the transactions are the same. First we check to see that we haven't received a null handle. This is a fatal error.

Next, we cast the rhs uvm_object into a command_transaction variable called compared_transaction_h. This is our first comparison; if this cast fails then these transactions are not the same and we set same to zero.

We set the same bit to 1'b1 if the three data fields in this object match the three data fields in the tested object, and if super.do_compare() returns a 1'b1.

Finally, we return the same bit.

The `convert2string()` Method

Like lions before them, our transaction needs a `convert2string()` method so we can print it to the screen:

```
58    function string convert2string();
59        string s;
60        s = $sformatf("A: %2h  B: %2h op: %s",
61                       A, B, op.name());
62        return s;
63    endfunction : convert2string
64
```

Figure 157: Converting the Command Transaction to a String

The `$sformatf()` method uses SystemVerilog format specifiers to convert our data to a string. The enumerated type value has a method called `name()` that returns the values as strings such as `add_op` and `no_op`.

Using Transactions

The move to transaction-based data requires that we modify almost every part of the TinyALU testbench. These are good modifications in that they simplify our code and make it easier to reuse.

Here is the list of changes:

- Step 1: Create a `result_transaction` class to hold results.

- Step 2: Create an `add_transaction` class that extends `command_transaction` and generates only add operations.

- Step 3: Rename `base_tester` to `tester` since it now works for all tests.

- Step 4: Modify the `command_monitor` to create a `command_transaction`.

- Step 5: Modify the `result_monitor` to create a `result_transaction`.

- Step 6: Modify the `scoreboard` to use the `result_transaction`'s `compare()` method.

- Step 7: Modify the `add_test` to use the `add_transaction`.

Clearly, life is easier if we design our testbench to use transactions from the start. But these are simple changes. Let's walk through them.

Step 1: Create a `result_transaction` Class to Hold Results

The `result_transaction` class is just like the `command_transaction` class, except that it has only one data element:

```
1  class result_transaction extends uvm_transaction;
2     `uvm_object_utils(result_transaction)
3
4     shortint result;
5
6     function bit do_compare(uvm_object rhs, uvm_comparer comparer);
7        result_transaction tested;
8        bit    same;
9
10       if (!$cast(tested,rhs))
```

Figure 158: The Result Transaction Class

The scoreboard will use the `do_compare()` method to compare predicted results to actual results.

Step 2: Create an `add_transaction` that Generates Only Add Operations

The `add_transaction` extends the `command_transaction` and provides a single randomization constraint:

```
1  class add_transaction extends command_transaction;
2     `uvm_object_utils(add_transaction)
3
4     constraint add_only {op == add_op;}
5
6     function new(string name="");super.new(name);endfunction
7  endclass : add_transaction
```

Figure 159: The Add Transaction

The `add_transaction` allows us to generate different stimulus without changing the `tester_h` object. The `tester_h` object will use the `add_transaction` in the same way as the `command_transaction`, but will receive only add operations.

Step 3: Rename the `base_tester` to `tester`...

Our previous design had two tester classes to implement two kinds of tests. The `base_tester` generated random stimulus, and the `add_tester` generated add operations with random operands. Now that we have an `add_transaction` we can collapse both tester classes into one. The `tester` class uses the `randomize()` method to generate operations:

```
23          command = command_transaction::type_id::create("command");
24          repeat (10) begin
25             assert(command.randomize());
26             command_port.put(command);
27          end
```

Figure 160: The Core of the `tester` Class

There are two keys to this code. The first is that we use the factory to create our `command_transaction`, so this transaction type can be overridden. The second is that we randomize the transaction, so constraints control the results we get. When we override the `command_transaction` using an `add_transaction`, we get only add operations.

Step 4: Modify the `command_monitor` to Create `command_transactions`

The `command_monitor` takes data from the BFM, packages it up, and sends it into the testbench. Now it sends a `command_transaction`:

```
19          function void write_to_monitor(byte A, byte B, operation_t op);
20             command_transaction cmd;
21             `uvm_info("COMMAND MONITOR",$sformatf("MONITOR: A: %2h  B: %2h  op: %s",
22                       A, B, op.name()), UVM_HIGH);
23             cmd = new("cmd");
24             cmd.A = A;
25             cmd.B = B;
26             cmd.op = op;
27             ap.write(cmd);
28          endfunction : write_to_monitor
29       endclass : command_monitor
```

Figure 161: Monitoring Commands

This code is similar to the previous code, but now we send an object.

Step 5: Modify the `result_monitor` to send a `result_transaction`

A simpler version of the command monitor:

```
17          function void write_to_monitor(shortint r);
18              result_transaction result_t;
19              result_t = new("result_t");
20              result_t.result = r;
21              ap.write(result_t);
22          endfunction : write_to_monitor
23
```

Figure 162: Monitoring Results with `result_transactions`

We're storing the number we get from the BFM into a `result_transaction` and sending that transaction to the testbench.

Step 6: Modify the `scoreboard` to use the `result_transaction's compare()` Method

Transaction-level simulation makes it easier to compare predicted and actual results. Both the result monitor and the predictor create `result_transaction` objects. If these are the same, then the result is okay:

```
36
37
38          do
39              if (!cmd_f.try_get(cmd))
40                  $fatal(1, "Missing command in self checker");
41          while ((cmd.op == no_op) || (cmd.op == rst_op));
42
43          predicted = predict_result(cmd);

51
52          if (!predicted.compare(t))
53              `uvm_error("SELF CHECKER", {"FAIL: ",data_str})
54          else
55              `uvm_info ("SELF CHECKER", {"PASS: ", data_str}, UVM_HIGH)
56
57          endfunction : write
58      endclass : scoreboard
```

Figure 163: A Transaction-Level Scoreboard

The `result_monitor` passes us an actual result called `t`. Then we get the corresponding command from the `command_monitor` and use the `predict_result()` method to create a predicted `result_transaction`.

We use `compare()` to see if we got the right result. The `scoreboard` is now much simpler.

Step 7: Modify the `add_test` to use the `add_transaction`

The `add_test` is identical to the `random_test`, except that we override the `command_transaction` with an `add_transaction`:

```
1   class add_test extends random_test;
2       `uvm_component_utils(add_test);
3
4   function void build_phase(uvm_phase phase);
5       tinyalu_transaction::type_id::set_type_override(add_transaction::get_type());
6       super.build_phase(phase);
7   endfunction : build_phase
8
```

Figure 164: Overriding `command_transaction` with `add_transaction`

The override causes the `tester` to create an `add_transaction` rather than a `command_transaction`, without modifying the `tester` code.

UVM Transaction Summary

In this chapter, we used `uvm_transactions` to pass data around the testbench. This allowed us to simplify our test components and even remove one class from the testbench (`add_tester`).

In our next chapter we will turn again to UVM hierarchy in our quest for reuse. We're going to recognize that all the classes associated with a given block or interface can be grouped together and reused in other testbenches that use that interface. We're going to learn about `uvm_agents`.

Chapter 22

UVM Agents

Modularity is a wonderful thing. Whether we use it to encapsulate blocks in hardware, subroutines in firmware, or objects in software, modularity hides complexity and improves life. Modularity also allows us to reuse tested functionality as IP in hardware, libraries in firmware, and class libraries in software.

The key to successful modularity is to support a strict and unchanging interface. Defining and preserving an interface allows users (and our future selves) to confidently use a modular component without worrying about its inner workings.

The UVM supports modularity with the concepts of *agents*, *configuration objects,* and the *configuration database*. Agents allow us to encapsulate similar objects, configuration objects allow us to store information the agent needs and the configuration database allows us to deliver configuration information to multiple instances of the same agent.

Consider our current testbench:

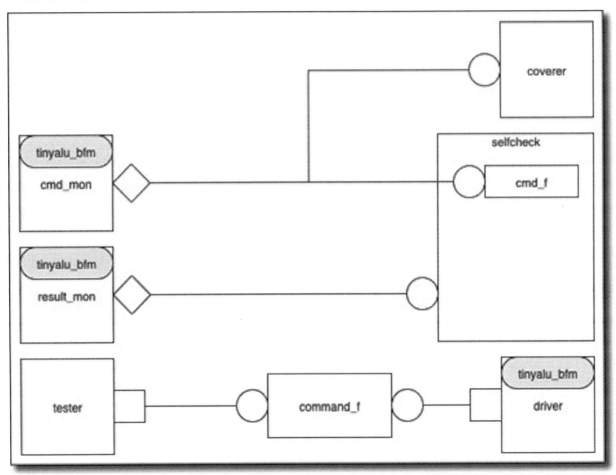

Figure 165: The Current TinyALU Testbench

This testbench generates stimulus, checks the results, and monitors our coverage. But it's ungainly. Consider the problems we'd have if there were multiple TinyALU's in the design. We'd have to copy all these objects and connections in order to reuse them. This is no way to support reuse.

We'll solve this problem by recognizing that all the objects in the current testbench either monitor or drive the TinyALU. We can make our lives easier if we encapsulate TinyALU related objects in a class called a `uvm_agent`, creating a TinyALU agent.

Here is our agent:

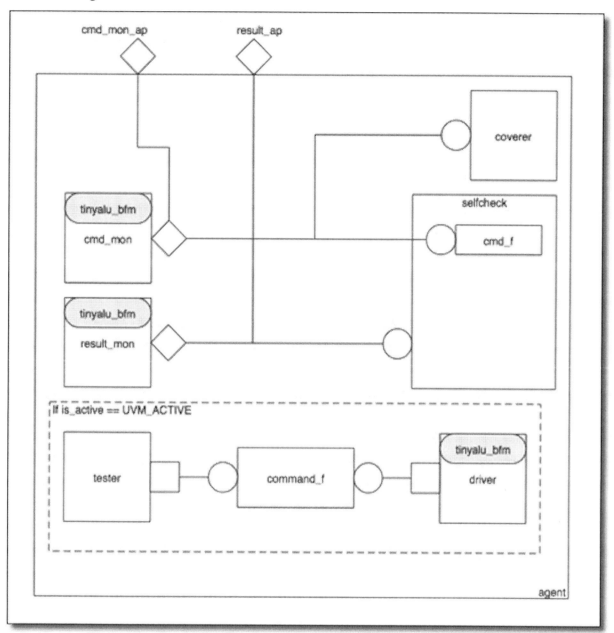

Figure 166: The TinyALU Agent

We've taken the same objects as above and encapsulated them within another `uvm_component` of type `uvm_agent`. We have all the same objects as we had in our testbench, connected in the same way. This way we won't have to redo the connections every time we want to work with another TinyALU.

We've also created a pair of top-level analysis ports to allow higher level components to monitor the traffic going through our agent. Meanwhile our `scoreboard_h` and `coverage_h` subscriptions remain unchanged.

The dashed line around the `tester_h`, `command_f`, and `driver_h` objects means that these are only instantiated when the user wants to generate stimulus. Without them, you can still use the agent to monitor the TinyALU.

Our TinyALU agent looks like this to the outside world:

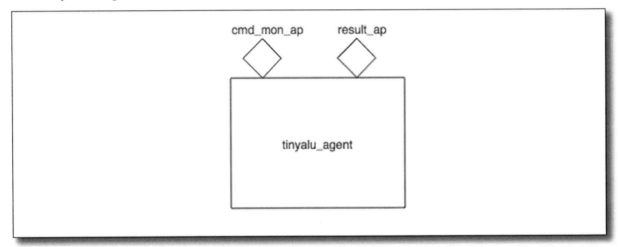

Figure 167: The TinyALU Agent Hides Details

Writing the TinyALU Agent

The `tinyalu_agent` class looks almost exactly like the `env` from the previous chapters. The difference is that we introduce a configuration class to transfer the BFM and control whether the agent creates stimulus.

The TinyALU agent contains all the components and FIFOs from our previous testbench. It also contains a configuration object:

```
1    class tinyalu_agent extends uvm_agent;
2       `uvm_component_utils(tinyalu_agent)
3
4       tinyalu_agent_config tinyalu_agent_config_h;
5
6       tester           tester_h;
7       driver           driver_h;
8       scoreboard       scoreboard_h;
9       coverage         coverage_h;
10      command_monitor  command_monitor_h;
11      result_monitor   result_monitor_h;
12
13      uvm_tlm_fifo      #(command_transaction) command_f;
14      uvm_analysis_port #(command_transaction) cmd_mon_ap;
15      uvm_analysis_port #(result_transaction) result_ap;
16
```

Figure 168: Agent Declarations

The `uvm_agent` provides the `is_active` data member and the `get_is_active()` method. The `is_active` data member is a variable of type `uvm_active_passive_enum`.

This enumerated type can take one of two values: UVM_ACTIVE or UVM_PASSIVE. The default is UVM_ACTIVE.

Since we expect to instantiate multiple identical agents, we need a way to pass them the handle to the TinyALU BFM and the value of the is_active variable. We do this with the tinyalu_agent_config class:

```
1   class tinyalu_agent_config;
2
3       virtual interface tinyalu_bfm bfm;
4       protected  uvm_active_passive_enum     is_active;
5
6       function new (virtual tinyalu_bfm bfm, uvm_active_passive_enum
7             is_active);
8          this.bfm = bfm;
9          this.is_active = is_active;
10      endfunction : new
11
12      function uvm_active_passive_enum get_is_active();
13          return is_active;
14      endfunction : get_is_active
15
16   endclass : tinyalu_agent_config
17
```

Figure 169: The TinyALU Agent Configuration Class

The TinyALU Agent retrieves the configuration object in its build_phase() method:

```
23   function void build_phase(uvm_phase phase);
24
25      if(!uvm_config_db #(tinyalu_agent_config)::get(this, "","config",
26                                          tinyalu_agent_config_h))
27        `uvm_fatal("AGENT", "Failed to get config object");
28      is_active = tinyalu_agent_config_h.get_is_active();
29
30      if (get_is_active() == UVM_ACTIVE) begin : make_stimulus
31         command_f = new("command_f", this);
32         tester_h    = tester::type_id::create( "tester_h",this);
33         driver_h    = driver::type_id::create("driver_h",this);
34      end
35
36      command_monitor_h = command_monitor::type_id::create("command_monitor_h",this);
37      result_monitor_h  = result_monitor::type_id::create("result_monitor_h",this);
38
39      coverage_h = coverage::type_id::create("coverage_h",this);
40      scoreboard_h = scoreboard::type_id::create("scoreboard_h",this);
41
42      cmd_mon_ap = new("cmd_mon_ap",this);
43      result_ap  = new("result_ap", this);
44
45   endfunction : build_phase
46
```

Figure 170: The TinyALU Agent Constructor

In this case the `uvm_config_db` passes us a handle to a `tinyalu_agent_config` object rather than a handle to a virtual interface. We pull the `is_active` value from the configuration object. As its name implies, the UVM designers expected this class to pass configuration objects around the testbench. The `uvm_config_db` usually passes configuration objects rather than BFMs.

The code above raises a question about creating multiple instances of the same class. If I pull my config object out of the `uvm_config_db` using the `"config"` string, then how do I differ from another instance of this object that also uses the `"config"` string? We'll see later that the `uvm_config_db` solves this problem.

Once we have our configuration data, we build the agent. Building the agent looks a lot like building the `env` from previous chapters, except that we have conditional instantiations based on the `is_active` variable.

Anyone who instantiates a TinyALU agent gets all the tools needed to drive stimulus to the TinyALU, monitor its results, calculate coverage, and check its behavior. Next we connect these objects to each other:

```
47  function void connect_phase(uvm_phase phase);
48      if (get_is_active() == UVM_ACTIVE) begin : make_stimulus
49          driver_h.command_port.connect(command_f.get_export);
50          tester_h.command_port.connect(command_f.put_export);
51      end
52
53      command_monitor_h.ap.connect(cmd_mon_ap);
54      result_monitor_h.ap.connect(result_ap);
55
56      command_monitor_h.ap.connect(scoreboard_h.cmd_f.analysis_export);
57      command_monitor_h.ap.connect(coverage_h.analysis_export);
58      result_monitor_h.ap.connect(scoreboard_h.analysis_export);
59
60  endfunction : connect_phase
```

Figure 171: The TinyALU Connect Phase

This method connects the objects to each other, and also presents analysis ports (`command_ap` and `result_ap`) to the top level as we see in Figure 167. The shaded lines above connect the lower level analysis ports (i.e., `command_monitor_h.ap`) to the top level analysis ports (i.e., `com_mon_ap`) by calling the lower level `connect()` methods and passing the top level analysis ports as arguments.

Now that we have an agent, let's use it in an example.

Using a UVM Agent

Imagine, if you will, a situation in which your boss finds out that you've replaced the `tester` module with a `tester` UVM component and is displeased. It turns out that he had written the tester module and is quite proud of it. He is especially proud of the get_op() method and won't stop talking about it.

You argue that the new system works well even though you didn't need the get_op() method. (You probably shouldn't have mentioned that!) Now he wants you to run two TinyALU simulations side-by-side to see which stimulus works better. You decide to appease him while updating your resume.

The Top-Level Module

In order to implement this benchmark, we instantiate two TinyALU modules and two TinyALU BFMs. We drive stimulus on one of the BFMs using our TinyALU agent, and we drive stimulus on the other using the tester_module. We'll use an agent on the second TinyALU to monitor results.

Here are the top-level module instantiations:

```
1   module top;
2       import uvm_pkg::*;
3       import    tinyalu_pkg::*;
4   `include "tinyalu_macros.svh"
5   `include "uvm_macros.svh"
6
7   tinyalu_bfm        class_bfm();
8
9   tinyalu class_dut (.A(class_bfm.A), .B(class_bfm.B), .op(class_bfm.op),
10                     .clk(class_bfm.clk), .reset_n(class_bfm.reset_n),
11                     .start(class_bfm.start), .done(class_bfm.done),
12                     .result(class_bfm.result));
13
14  tinyalu_bfm        module_bfm();
15
16  tinyalu module_dut (.A(module_bfm.A), .B(module_bfm.B), .op(module_bfm.op),
17                     .clk(module_bfm.clk), .reset_n(module_bfm.reset_n),
18                     .start(module_bfm.start), .done(module_bfm.done),
19                     .result(module_bfm.result));
20
21  tinyalu_tester_module stim_module(module_bfm);
22
```

Figure 172: Dual TinyALU Top Level

We have two DUTS (class_dut and module_dut) and two tinyalu_bfm interfaces (class_bfm and module_bfm.) We also have a tinyalu_tester_module connected to module_bfm.

Next we connect the BFMs to the testbench.

Modularity works best when users don't know what's going on inside a module or object, but instead work through a clearly defined interface. Clearly defined interfaces free the user from thinking about implementation details and allow the user to focus on top-level thoughts.

In the case of this dual TinyALU testbench we don't want the user to worry about whether we've used agents inside our testbench to implement the test. Instead we want to user to follow simple external steps that hide our testbench.

Here is our user's interface to the dual TinyALU testbench:

```
23   initial begin
24     uvm_config_db #(virtual tinyalu_bfm)::set(null, "*", "class_bfm", class_bfm);
25     uvm_config_db #(virtual tinyalu_bfm)::set(null, "*", "module_bfm", module_bfm);
26     run_test("dual_test");
27   end
28
29   endmodule : top
```

Figure 173: Invoking the Testbench

The code uses the `uvm_config_db` to pass the `class_bfm` using the "class_bfm" string and the `module_bfm` using the "module_bfm" string. Then the code calls `run_test("dual_test")` and we handle the rest. The code's author doesn't need to worry about the details of where these BFMs will go. We'll handle that, and as we'll see we'll maintain modularity throughout our design.

The `dual_test` class

The testbench's top-level module stored the `class_bfm` and `module_bfm` in the `uvm_config_db` with no notion of how these interfaces would be used inside the test. The `dual_test` class's job is to take those raw BFMs and store them in a configuration object for the environment.

This notion of using a configuration object at each level of the hierarchy makes it possible to reuse the classes in our testbench because the configuration object acts as a clean interface. If we instantiate and populate a configuration object, we know that the class that uses that object will be happy.

The `dual_test` class only instantiates one object, the `env`. Therefore we need to instantiate the `env`'s configuration object and pass it to the `env` using the `uvm_config_db`. Here is the `env`'s configuration class:

```
1   class env_config;
2     virtual tinyalu_bfm class_bfm;
3     virtual tinyalu_bfm module_bfm;
4
5     function new(virtual tinyalu_bfm class_bfm, virtual tinyalu_bfm module_bfm);
6        this.class_bfm = class_bfm;
7        this.module_bfm = module_bfm;
8     endfunction : new
9   endclass : env_config
```

Figure 174: The `env`'s Configuration Class

The `env_config` class stores the two `tinyalu_bfm` interfaces in the testbench. We ensure that the user will populate the class's data members by placing them in the constructor. Now the simulator will cough up a syntax error if the user forgets to provide the correct values.

The `dual_top` test contains only `build_phase()`:

```
10
11  function void build_phase(uvm_phase phase);
12
13    virtual tinyalu_bfm class_bfm, module_bfm;
14    env_config env_config_h;
15
16    if(!uvm_config_db #(virtual tinyalu_bfm)::get(this, "","class_bfm", class_bfm))
17      `uvm_fatal("DUAL TEST", "Failed to get CLASS BFM");
18    if(!uvm_config_db #(virtual tinyalu_bfm)::get(this, "","module_bfm", module_bfm))
19      `uvm_fatal("DUAL TEST", "Failed to get MODULE BFM");
20
21    env_config_h = new(.class_bfm(class_bfm), .module_bfm(module_bfm));
22
23    uvm_config_db #(env_config)::set(this, "env_h*", "config", env_config_h);
24
25    env_h = env::type_id::create("env_h",this);
26  endfunction : build_phase
27
28
```

Figure 175: Building Using a Config Object

The build phase gets the `class_bfm` and `module_bfm` out of the `uvm_config_db` and uses them to instantiate the `env_config_h` object. Then it stores the `env_config_h` object back in the `uvm_config_db`.

The `uvm_config_db::set` call in this example is different from any we've seen before. All our previous `set()` calls were from `initial` blocks in modules. This call is being made from within the UVM hierarchy. As a result, we can use the `uvm_config_db`'s filtering functionality.

The call has two big differences. The first is that we pass the `this` variable to set the context for storing our information. Next we pass a string that tells the `uvm_config_db` who can see this data. In this case, we limit the reader to the `env_h` class instantiated within this test. This is redundant here since we instantiate only one object. We'll use this filtering functionality to better effect inside the `env`.

The TinyALU Environment

In our previous testbenches the `env` class served simply as a convenient place to instantiate our components. Now that we're working with multiple agents, the `env` class has a bigger job; it creates configuration objects for the various agent instances and stores them someplace the agents can get to them.

This class uses the hierarchical filtering functionality in the `uvm_config_db` to its full extent. Remember that the `tinyalu_agent` class gets its configuration object from the database

(Figure 170) using the "config" string.)The question is, what do we do when multiple instances of the same agent want to access the database with the same string?

The answer is that the uvm_config_db allows us to apply different configuration objects to different parts of the UVM hierarchy. The env gets the configuration data from the uvm_config_db, creates config objects for each tinyalu_agent instance and stores the config objects so that each instance sees the correct object:

```
17
18    if(!uvm_config_db #(env_config)::get(this, "","config", env_config_h))
19      `uvm_fatal("RANDOM TEST", "Failed to get CLASS BFM");
20
21    class_config_h  = new(.bfm(env_config_h.class_bfm),  .is_active(UVM_ACTIVE));
22    module_config_h = new(.bfm(env_config_h.module_bfm), .is_active(UVM_PASSIVE));
23
24    uvm_config_db #(tinyalu_agent_config)::set(this, "class_tinyalu_agent_h*",
25                                    "config", class_config_h);
26
27    uvm_config_db #(tinyalu_agent_config)::set(this, "module_tinyalu_agent_h*",
28                                    "config", module_config_h);
29
```

Figure 176: Storing Configuration Objects in the Hierarchy

We've created two configuration objects, one for each agent. The class_config_h holds the class_bfm and sets is_active to UVM_ACTIVE because the agent will generate stimulus. The module_config_h object holds the module_bfm and sets is_active to UVM_PASSIVE because our boss's module will provide the stimulus.

We finish the job by instantiating the agents using the names that match the set() calls above:

```
31
32    class_tinyalu_agent_h  = new("class_tinyalu_agent_h",this);
33    module_tinyalu_agent_h = new("module_tinyalu_agent_h",this);
34
```

Figure 177: Creating Agents to Match the Config

Now the different instances of the tinyalu_agent will get different tinyalu_agent_config objects.

UVM Agent Summary

In this chapter we learned how to encapsulate components into a UVM agent class. This encapsulation allows us to easily reuse our testbench components, or create multiple instances of the same components. We also learned how to create active agents that generate stimulus, and passive agents that only monitor our interfaces. Modularity made life easy for us.

This pattern of encapsulating behavior in an object is recursive if each level of hierarchy has a clearly defined configuration object. We could instantiate two env classes to simulate four TinyALU's with only minor modifications.

Only one thing is left to do to create truly reusable and modular testbenches. You may have noticed an odd thing about our `agent` class. Though we might want to run many different kinds of stimulus through our agent, the built-in `tester` provides only one default set of stimulus. We can control this to some degree by overriding the `command_transaction`, but this is just a way of working around a hokey problem.

What we'd really like to do is to have a way to give an agent different commands so that it will generate different kinds of stimulus. We want to separate the stimulus from the testbench structure. We will do that in our next chapter on UVM sequences.

Chapter 23

UVM Sequences

Throughout the *UVM Primer* we have been teasing apart pieces of testbench functionality to create smaller and simpler design units. This approach delivers adaptable code that makes your testbench stronger as it grows and can be reused in future testbenches.

In the previous chapter, UVM Agents, we focused on structure. We took all the components associated with the TinyALU and encapsulated them in a single component that we could easily reuse.

In the chapter on UVM Transactions, we focused on data. We created classes and objects that made it easy to create, compare, and transport data. We separated the data classes from the structure classes.

In this chapter, we're going to address the final muddling point between data and structure: test stimulus. For although we have separated data from structure, we have not separated data stimulus from structure. This is poor testbench design, and our `tester` class is the problem.

The `tester` creates new transactions and feeds them into the testbench. This means the tester is doing two things: choosing the order of the transactions and feeding them to the testbench. This makes reuse a problem. A future designer (or future you) might think the `tester` is the perfect solution to the problem of creating new transactions, but will not be able to use it because the `tester` has the side effect of determining stimulus.

We can override the transaction type to control data randomization, but we must override the entire tester class to change the number of transactions and the way they are sent. This is like swapping out your car's steering wheel whenever you chose a different destination.

Good testbenches separate the order of the transactions (the test stimulus) from the testbench structure. The structure should remain unchanged regardless of the order of transactions. We're going to demonstrate how to do this with the TinyALU by creating three tests:

- The Fibonacci Test uses our TinyALU to calculate the Fibonacci Sequence

- The Full Random Test uses constrained random data to meet our functional coverage goals

- The Interleaved Test combines the Fibonacci test and the Full Random test into one stream of stimulus

These tests demonstrate why we want to separate stimulus generation from structure. While we could create a Fibonacci tester and a Full Random tester, we'd have to create a whole new tester to combine them. If we added more tests and more combinations, we'd have an explosion of tester classes. These would be hard to maintain.

UVM sequences separate stimulus from the testbench structure. They allow us to create one testbench structure and then run different data through it, thus completing our journey through the UVM.

We're going to learn about UVM sequences by converting our current transaction-level testbench into one that uses sequences. This process requires seven steps:

- Step 1: Create a TinyALU Sequence Item to carry our data.

- Step 2: Replace the `tester` with a `uvm_sequencer`.

- Step 3: Upgrade the `driver` to support sequences.

- Step 4: Instantiate the `driver` and `sequencer` in the environment and connect them.

- Step 5: Write UVM sequences.

- Step 6: Write a test that starts the sequences using the sequencer.

Each of these steps is easy, and by the time we reach the end of them we'll have a complete and adaptable testbench.

Step 1: Create the TinyALU Sequence Item

Two chapters ago we learned about the `uvm_transaction` class. The UVM extends that class to create the `uvm_sequence_item` class. The `uvm_sequence_item` carries data from `uvm_sequences` through the `uvm_sequencer` to a `uvm_driver`.

First, convert our `command_transaction` to a `sequence_item`:

```
class sequence_item extends uvm_sequence_item;
    `uvm_object_utils(sequence_item);

    function new(string name = "");
        super.new(name);
    endfunction : new

    rand byte unsigned        A;
    rand byte unsigned        B;
    rand operation_t          op;
    shortint  unsigned        result;

    constraint op_con {op dist {no_op := 1, add_op := 5, and_op:=5,
                          xor_op:=5,mul_op:=5, rst_op:=1};}
```

Figure 178: The TinyALU Sequence Item

The `sequence_item` class is exactly the same as the `command_transaction` class except for two things:

- We extended `uvm_sequence_item` instead of `uvm_transaction`.

- We added the `result` into the `tinyalu_item` for reasons that will become clear later.

The rest of the class is identical to the transaction, and so we'll move on to step 2.

Step 2: Replace the `tester` with a `uvm_sequencer`

In our previous example, we encapsulated all the TinyALU components in a single component called a TinyALU agent. Since this chapter is not devoted to agents, we're going to go back to a testbench in which all our components are instantiated in the `env` class.

Our current version of `env` instantiates an object called `tester_h` of class `tester`. As we said before, the `tester` is an ill-conceived class. It tries to do too much, and so it becomes hard to maintain and reuse. Worst of all, we have to write it ourselves.

All we want the tester to do is deliver sequence items to the driver. We want some other part of the testbench to decide on the order of the sequence items. So it's really not correct to call the class a `tester` anymore. Instead, let's rename the class and call it a `sequencer`.

The `sequencer` class takes `sequence_items` from a sequence and passes them on to a driver. The UVM provides us with a `uvm_sequencer` base class. We use it like this:

```
13    `include "sequence_item.svh"
14    typedef uvm_sequencer #(sequence_item) sequencer;
15    sequencer sequencer_h;
16
```

Figure 179: Declaring the Sequencer

We define all our classes and types in a package called `tinyalu_pkg`. In the above line we define the `sequencer` class to be a `uvm_sequencer` class parameterized to accept our `sequence_items`. Using a `typedef` to set the parameterization on a class makes it easy to use that class name later in the design.

Step 3: Upgrade the Driver to Support Sequences

Throughout the primer we've been using the name "driver" in a generic way to talk about an object that interacted with the BFM. We implemented our driver by extending `uvm_component` and instantiating the driver in our environment.

The UVM has a more specific concept for the word "driver" than ours. It defines a class called a `uvm_driver` that extends `uvm_component` and interacts with a `uvm_sequencer`. We upgrade our driver by extending `uvm_driver` and by modifying its `run_phase()` method.

First we extend `uvm_driver` and parameterize it to work with the `sequence_item`:

```
1    class driver extends uvm_driver #(sequence_item);
2        `uvm_component_utils(driver)
3
4        virtual tinyalu_bfm bfm;
5
6        function void build_phase(uvm_phase phase);
7            if(!uvm_config_db #(virtual tinyalu_bfm)::get(null, "*","bfm", bfm))
```

Figure 180: Extending the `uvm_driver` Class

When we extend `uvm_driver` we inherit the `seq_item_port` object and all its functionality. Now we modify the run phase to use our new `seq_item_port`:

```
10
11      task run_phase(uvm_phase phase);
12          sequence_item cmd;
13
14          forever begin : cmd_loop
15              shortint unsigned result;
16              seq_item_port.get_next_item(cmd);
17              bfm.send_op(cmd.A, cmd.B, cmd.op, result);
18              cmd.result = result;
19              seq_item_port.item_done();
20          end : cmd_loop
21      endtask : run_phase
```

Figure 181: The Driver Run Phase

The run phase calls the `get_next_item()` method on the `seq_item_port` object. This method blocks until the sequencer puts data into the port and then gives us a `sequence_item` object in `cmd`.

Once we have the command, we call the `send_op` task in the BFM and get back the result. Then, we store the result in the `cmd` object. We do this to return the data to whoever called us. We assume that the code that passed us the `cmd` still has a handle to it and that by storing the data in the command we are returning it to the caller.[25]

We call the `item_done()` method on the `seq_item_port` object to tell the sequencer that it can send us another sequence item.

---

[25] We have intentionally violated the Manual Obligatory Object Copy On Write (MOOCOW) rule here. We've modified the `cmd` without copying it. But it's okay, because the person who sent us the `cmd` wants us to modify the object and will not be surprised by the change.

Step 4: Instantiate the Driver and Sequencer in the Environment and Connect Them

We replace the `tester` in the `env` with a `sequencer` and connect it to the driver class:

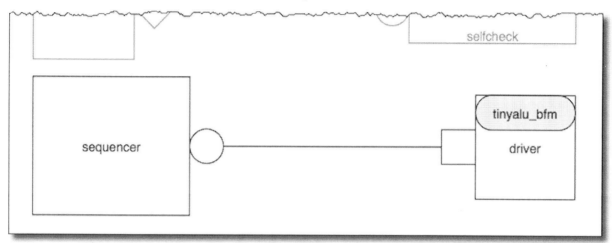

Figure 182: Replacing the Tester with a Sequencer

Our new environment has two changes:

- We replaced the `tester` with a `uvm_sequencer`.

- The sequencer doesn't need a FIFO to connect to the driver. Our driver expects to connect to a sequencer and can do it directly. We'll see how next.

Here are the key pieces of our new `env` code. Declare the sequencer and other components:

```
1    class env extends uvm_env;
2        `uvm_component_utils(env);
3
4        sequencer        sequencer_h;
5        coverage         coverage_h;
6        scoreboard       scoreboard_h;
7        driver           driver_h;
8        command_monitor  command_monitor_h;
9        result_monitor   result_monitor_h;
10
11       function new (string name, uvm_component parent);
```

Figure 183: The TinyALU Environment Declarations

Instantiate `sequencer` taking care to pass the correct name in the constructor:

```
15       function void build_phase(uvm_phase phase);
16           // stimulus
17           sequencer_h  = new("sequencer_h",this);
18           driver_h     = driver::type_id::create("driver_h",this);
```

Figure 184: The TinyALU Environment Build Phase Instantiates a Sequencer

Connect the sequencer to the driver:

```
28    function void connect_phase(uvm_phase phase);
30      driver_h.seq_item_port.connect(sequencer_h.seq_item_export);
```

Figure 185: Connecting the Sequencer to the Driver

We did not need a TLM FIFO to connect the sequencer and the driver. The `uvm_sequencer` comes equipped with an object called a `seq_item_export` (analogous to the `put_export` and `analysis_exports` we saw earlier). We connect the driver to the sequencer by calling the `connect()` method on the driver's `seq_item_port`.

Wait. What? A `seq_item_port`? Where did that come from?

That brings us to our next step: upgrading our driver.

And that's all there is to upgrading our testbench to handle sequences. We're ready to create a UVM sequence and use it to send sequence items.

Step 5: Writing UVM Sequences

The `uvm_sequence` class sits outside the UVM hierarchy (it has no `parent` argument in its constructor) but can feed data into the UVM hierarchy through the `uvm_sequencer`. Classes that extend `uvm_sequence` inherit three things that allow them to feed data to a sequencer:

- `m_sequencer`—This data member holds a handle to the sequencer that takes our sequence items.

- `task body()`—The UVM launches this task when it starts our sequence.

- `start_item()`/`finish_item()` method pair—These two methods get control of the sequencer and send it a sequence item.

We define `uvm_sequences` by extending `uvm_sequence`, parameterizing it to the `sequence_item` we want, and writing a `body()` method to create sequence_items and send them to the sequencer. Let's learn how to do this by generating the famous Fibonacci sequence.

The Fibonacci sequence creates numbers by adding two numbers to create the next in the sequence. The numbers in the sequence show up throughout nature, for example in the distance of the planets from the sun and the number of petals in each row of a daisy. Here are the Fibonacci numbers that can be stored in eight bits:

0   1   1   2   3   5   8   13   21   34   55   89   144   233

Our sequence generates these numbers using the adder in the TinyALU.

Here is the code:

```
1    class fibonacci_sequence extends uvm_sequence #(sequence_item);
2        `uvm_object_utils(fibonacci_sequence);
3
4        function new(string name = "fibonacci");
5            super.new(name);
6        endfunction : new
7
```

Figure 186: Extending `uvm_sequence` to Create the Fibonacci Sequence

We extend the `uvm_sequence` and parameterize it so that it will work with a `sequence_item`. We use the `uvm_object_utils()` macro instead of the `uvm_component_utils()` macro that we use with `uvm_components`. We also use a single-argument constructor.

We do all our work in the `body()` task. The UVM calls the `body()` task when someone starts the sequence:

```
9        task body();
10           byte unsigned n_minus_2=0;
11           byte unsigned n_minus_1=1;
12           sequence_item command;
13
14           command = sequence_item::type_id::create("command");
15
16           start_item(command);
17           command.op = rst_op;
18           finish_item(command);
```

Figure 187: The Fibonacci Command Object in Action

The snippet above demonstrates the basics of a `uvm_sequence body()` task. On line 12 we declare a variable to hold our `sequence_item` object. Then we instantiate the command object.

The `start_item()` method blocks until the `uvm_sequencer` is ready to accept our sequence item. Once we unblock, we know that the testbench is ready to receive our command. In this case the command is a simple reset.

The `finish_item()` method blocks until the driver completes the command. Once we're through the `finish_item()`, we know that the TinyALU is reset and ready for Fibonacci action:

```
20          `uvm_info("FIBONACCI", " Fib(01) = 00", UVM_MEDIUM);
21          `uvm_info("FIBONACCI", " Fib(02) = 01", UVM_MEDIUM);
22          for(int ff = 3; ff<=14; ff++) begin
23            start_item(command);
24            command.A = n_minus_2;
25            command.B = n_minus_1;
26            command.op = add_op;
27            finish_item(command);
28            n_minus_2 = n_minus_1;
29            n_minus_1 = command.result;
30            `uvm_info("FIBONACCI", $sformatf("Fib(%02d) = %02d", ff, n_minus_1),
31                      UVM_MEDIUM);
32          end
33        endtask : body
34      endclass : fibonacci_sequence
35
```

Figure 188: Cranking Out the Fibonacci Sequence

The Fibonacci loop above demonstrates how we read results back from the DUT. We call `start_item()` to wait for the sequencer. Then we load our two previous Fibonacci numbers into the command along with the `add_op` command to the ALU. Then we call the `finish_item()` method to wait for the driver to call `item_done()`. We block until the operation is complete.

Remember that the driver wrote the result into the command transaction (Figure 181**Error! Reference source not found.**.) We kept a handle to the transaction, so we can read the result after we return from the `finish_item()` task.

And that's all there is to writing a sequence. Next we'll look at our test to see how to start a sequence.

Step 6: Write a Test that Starts a Sequence on the Sequencer

All the tests in our testbench share the same `build_phase()` and `end_of_elaboration_phase()` methods, so we'll create a base class with those methods and extend it to create our tests:

```
virtual class tinyalu_base_test extends uvm_test;

    env      env_h;
    sequencer sequencer_h;

    function void build_phase(uvm_phase phase);
        env_h = env::type_id::create("env_h",this);
    endfunction : build_phase

    function void end_of_elaboration_phase(uvm_phase phase);
        sequencer_h = env_h.sequencer_h;
    endfunction : end_of_elaboration_phase

    function new (string name, uvm_component parent);
        super.new(name,parent);
    endfunction : new

endclass
```

Figure 189: The TinyALU Base Test

The `end_of_elaboration_phase()` method copies the sequencer from the environment. Now any test that extends the base test will have a handle to the sequencer.

The Fibonacci Test

The Fibonacci test instantiates a `fibonacci_sequence` and starts it using the sequencer:

```
class fibonacci_test extends tinyalu_base_test;
    `uvm_component_utils(fibonacci_test);

    task run_phase(uvm_phase phase);
    fibonacci_sequence fibonacci;
    fibonacci = new("fibonacci");

    phase.raise_objection(this);
    fibonacci.start(sequencer_h);
    phase.drop_objection(this);

    endtask : run_phase
```

Figure 190: The Fibonacci Test

All `uvm_sequences` have a `start()` method that takes a `uvm_sequencer` as an argument and returns once the sequence has completed. In this case the `start()` method returns once we've generated the Fibonacci sequence. Here is the output from this test:

```
103    # UVM_INFO @ 0: reporter [RNTST] Running test fibonacci_test...
104    # UVM_INFO <snipped> [FIBONACCI]  Fib(01) = 00
105    # UVM_INFO <snipped> [FIBONACCI]  Fib(02) = 01
106    # UVM_INFO <snipped> [FIBONACCI] Fib(03) = 01
107    # UVM_INFO <snipped> [FIBONACCI] Fib(04) = 02
108    # UVM_INFO <snipped> [FIBONACCI] Fib(05) = 03
109    # UVM_INFO <snipped> [FIBONACCI] Fib(06) = 05
110    # UVM_INFO <snipped> [FIBONACCI] Fib(07) = 08
111    # UVM_INFO <snipped> [FIBONACCI] Fib(08) = 13
112    # UVM_INFO <snipped> [FIBONACCI] Fib(09) = 21
113    # UVM_INFO <snipped> [FIBONACCI] Fib(10) = 34
114    # UVM_INFO <snipped> [FIBONACCI] Fib(11) = 55
115    # UVM_INFO <snipped> [FIBONACCI] Fib(12) = 89
116    # UVM_INFO <snipped> [FIBONACCI] Fib(13) = 144
117    # UVM_INFO <snipped> [FIBONACCI] Fib(14) = 233
```

Figure 191: Generating Fibonacci Numbers

We passed a sequencer to the `fibonacci_sequence`'s `start()` method and got Fibonacci numbers. Now that we have a sequencer in our testbench, we can run any combination of stimulus through it without having to modify the structure.

Given a handle to the sequencer, we can launch any sequences in any order by calling their `start()` methods and passing them the sequencer. But we don't have to pass a sequencer to `start()`. Here, the UVM gives us yet **another** opportunity to use the word "virtual" by naming a sequencer-free sequence a **virtual sequence**.

Virtual Sequences

Our Fibonacci sequence was a simple, one-shot kind of sequence. It ran through its stimulus and was done. However, we often need to mix and match a variety of behaviors by running several sequences either serially or in parallel. Let's fully test our TinyALU with the `runall_sequence`. The `runall_sequence` is a **virtual** sequence. It is called without a sequencer. Instead, it gets a handle to the sequencer and uses it to call other sequences.

The `uvm_pkg` provides an object called `uvm_top` that solves this problem. The `uvm_top` object is of type `uvm_root` and it provides access to several utilities. One of these utilities is the `find()` method.

The `uvm_top.find()` method takes the name of a component's instance as a string and returns a handle to the component. We can use a wildcard in our find string to allow us to find the component without knowing the whole hierarchy.

The `uvm_top.find()` method returns an object of type `uvm_component`, so we need to cast the return value from that base class to the class we want. In our case, we're going to get the

180

handle of the sequencer by passing "`*.env_h.sequencer_h`" to the `uvm_top.find()` method and casting the returned value to a variable of type `sequencer`.

Here is the `runall_sequence` class:

```
1   class runall_sequence extends uvm_sequence #(uvm_sequence_item);
2       `uvm_object_utils(runall_sequence);
3
4       protected reset_sequence reset;
5       protected maxmult_sequence maxmult;
6       protected random_sequence random;
7       protected sequencer sequencer_h;
8       protected uvm_component uvm_component_h;
9
10      function new(string name = "runall_sequence");
11          super.new(name);
12
13          uvm_component_h =  uvm_top.find("*.env_h.sequencer_h");
14
15          if (uvm_component_h == null)
16              `uvm_fatal("RUNALL SEQUENCE", "Failed to get the sequencer")
17
18          if (!$cast(sequencer_h, uvm_component_h))
19              `uvm_fatal("RUNALL SEQUENCE", "Failed to cast from uvm_component_h.")
```

Figure 192: Top of Virtual `runall` Sequence

The code above breaks the process of getting a handle into three steps for teaching purposes. First we use `uvm_top.find()` to get a `uvm_component` handle to the sequencer. Then we test to see that we got a handle. If we didn't, it means there is a misspelling in our string. Once we have a handle we cast it to be a `sequencer` handle while testing to see if the cast succeeded. If the cast fails it means that we got a handle to a component that is not a `sequencer`.

The `runall_sequence` uses three other sequences to do its job: a `reset_sequence`, `maxmult_sequence`, and `random_sequence`. We instantiated the three sequences in the constructor. Now we'll launch them in our `body()` method:

```
21
22          reset = reset_sequence::type_id::create("reset");
23          maxmult = maxmult_sequence::type_id::create("maxmult");
24          random = random_sequence::type_id::create("random");
25      endfunction : new
26
27      task body();
28          reset.start(sequencer_h);
29          maxmult.start(sequencer_h);
30          random.start(sequencer_h);
31      endtask : body
32
33      endclass : runall_sequence
34
```

Figure 193: Virtual Sequence Body Method

The `runall_sequence` virtual sequence launches each of the other sequences in order. First it resets the TinyALU, then it does the maximum multiplication possible, finally it runs a randomized sequence.

Launching the Virtual Sequence without a Sequencer

The UVM Developers call virtual sequences "virtual" because they can be launched without a sequencer. Here is an example of launching a sequence using no sequencer. The example is from a test called `full_test`:

```
1   class full_test extends tinyalu_base_test;
2       `uvm_component_utils(full_test);
3
4       runall_sequence runall_seq;
5
6       task run_phase(uvm_phase phase);
7           phase.raise_objection(this);
8           runall_seq.start(null);
9           phase.drop_objection(this);
10      endtask : run_phase
11
```

Figure 194: Starting a Sequence without a Sequencer

We launch the `runall_seq` without using a sequencer by passing `null` to the `start()` method. As we saw above, `runall_sequence` has its own way of getting the sequencer.

Virtual Sequences with Parallel Threads

We often need to run sequences in parallel threads. We might do this to see if we can create collisions between data coming in on different ports. We create parallel threads using SystemVerilog's `fork`/`join` construct. The fork statement launches things in different threads and the join statement blocks until all the things have completed. The "things" can be SystemVerilog statements, task calls, or sequence starts.

Let's create a sequence that runs the random sequence at the same time as the Fibonacci sequence.

Here is the test that launches the parallel run:

```
1   class parallel_test extends tinyalu_base_test;
2      `uvm_component_utils(parallel_test);
3
4      parallel_sequence parallel_h;
5
6      function new(string name, uvm_component parent);
7         super.new(name,parent);
8         parallel_h = new("parallel");
9      endfunction : new
10
11     task run_phase(uvm_phase phase);
12        phase.raise_objection(this);
13        parallel_h.start(sequencer_h);
14        phase.drop_objection(this);
15     endtask : run_phase
16
```

Figure 195: Launching a Virtual Sequence Using a Sequencer

In this example, we've passed the sequencer to the top-level sequence. It will use the sequencer when it launches the `fibonacci_sequence` and the `short_random_sequence`.

Here is the `parallel_sequence`:

```
1   class parallel_sequence extends uvm_sequence #(uvm_sequence_item);
2       `uvm_object_utils(parallel_sequence);
3
4       protected reset_sequence reset;
5       protected short_random_sequence short_random;
6       protected fibonacci_sequence fibonacci;
7
8       function new(string name = "parallel_sequence");
9           super.new(name);
10          reset = reset_sequence::type_id::create("reset");
11          fibonacci = fibonacci_sequence::type_id::create("fibonacci");
12          short_random = short_random_sequence::type_id::create("short_random");
13      endfunction : new
14
15      task body();
16          reset.start(m_sequencer);
17          fork
18              fibonacci.start(m_sequencer);
19              short_random.start(m_sequencer);
20          join
21      endtask : body
22  endclass : parallel_sequence
23
```

Figure 196: Launching Parallel Sequences Using `m_sequencer`

The `start()` method stores its argument in a data member called `m_sequencer`, then calls the `body()` task. You use `m_sequencer` to call `start()` on other sequences as we've done above.

We call `start()` on the `reset_sequence` first. Then we use the `fork/join` construct to launch the `fibonacci_sequence` and `short_random_sequence` in parallel. The sequencer will arbitrate between them to make sure that both sequences get their chance to use the DUT.

The `uvm_sequencer` supports a variety of arbitration schemes. The default is FIFO, which will interleave the sequence items as we'll see when we run the simulation. Here it goes:

```
1   UVM_INFO @ 0: reporter [RNTST] Running test parallel_test...
2   UVM_INFO <snip> [FIBONACCI]  Fib(01) = 00
3   UVM_INFO <snip> [FIBONACCI]  Fib(02) = 01
4   UVM_INFO <snip> [SHORT RANDOM] random command: A: 22 B: 21 op: and_op = 0000
5   UVM_INFO <snip> [FIBONACCI] Fib(03) = 01
6   UVM_INFO <snip> [SHORT RANDOM] random command: A: e4 B: 22 op: rst_op = 0000
7   UVM_INFO <snip> [FIBONACCI] Fib(04) = 02
8   UVM_INFO <snip> [SHORT RANDOM] random command: A: 93 B: ed op: add_op = 0000
9   UVM_INFO <snip> [FIBONACCI] Fib(05) = 03
10  UVM_INFO <snip> [SHORT RANDOM] random command: A: 83 B: 7f op: add_op = 0000
11  UVM_INFO <snip> [FIBONACCI] Fib(06) = 05
12  UVM_INFO <snip> [SHORT RANDOM] random command: A: b2 B: 71 op: xor_op = 0000
13  UVM_INFO <snip> [FIBONACCI] Fib(07) = 08
```

Figure 197: Interleaved Operations from Parallel Sequences

We see the Fibonacci operations interleaved with the random operations from the random sequence. We've tested the fact that there is no interference between the operations. The Fibonacci sequence continues as always.

UVM Sequences Summary

In this chapter, we learned about the last piece of UVM technology: UVM sequences. Sequences allow us to separate test stimulus from testbench structure, mixing and matching different stimulus to create a variety of tests.

We learned how to convert a testbench into a sequence-driven testbench, how to extend the correct classes to use sequences, and how to transfer data from the DUT back into our testbench. Then we saw how to use sequences to launch other sequences and how we can launch sequences in parallel if we wish.

We also saw the power of being able to create a variety of stimulus behaviors and then mix and match them in tests and sequences.

Chapter 24

Onward with the UVM

It has been said that earning a black belt in the martial art Aikido shows only that one is ready to start learning Aikido in earnest. The same can be said for learning all the material in this ***UVM Primer***.

The Primer has taught you the mechanics of the UVM. You've learned how to create an object-oriented testbench by defining classes, instantiating objects, and connecting them together. You've learned how to break a testbench down into small, easily reused pieces, and you've learned how to drive the testbench with stimulus from UVM sequences.

So what's next?

Next you start down the road of using object-oriented programming techniques to create testbenches. Fortunately, you are not alone on this road. The UVM is a rich and powerful development tool. Once you start using object-oriented programming for testbenches, you will unlock a world of new techniques and approaches.

Enjoy the UVM.

Index

Made in the USA
Lexington, KY
01 March 2015